FIVE PLAYS

Comedies and Tragicomedies

ALSO BY FEDERICO GARCÍA LORCA

Selected Poems

Three Tragedies

About the author

GARCÍA LORCA

by Edwin Honig

FIVE PLAYS
Comedies and Tragicomedies

by Federico García Lorca

*Translated by James Graham-Lujan and
Richard L. O'Connell*

A *New Directions* BOOK

PUBLISHER'S NOTE

Three plays in this volume—*The Shoemaker's Prodigious Wife, The Love of Don Perlimplín,* and *Doña Rosita, The Spinster*—were previously published in English in *From Lorca's Theatre* (Charles Scribner's Sons, 1941). The translations of that edition, however, have been considerably revised to conform to the Spanish texts established for the well-edited Aguilar *Obras Completas* in its successive editions published in Madrid. Two lines which were omitted from the Aguilar texts, however, but which appeared in the previous *Obras Completas* published by Losada in Buenos Aires, have been translated and inserted here. Further revisions are the result of the experience of many productions of these plays, several directed by the translators themselves. Once the melodies for the songs in the plays were ascertained, the translations of the songs themselves had to be revised so that they could be sung to the music, which appears as an appendix to the book. The publisher takes full responsibility for the revised songs.

The plays are arranged chronologically, except that *The Butterfly's Evil Spell,* which was the first to be written and produced, appears at the end as a kind of appendix. This is because it is incomplete and because it is an early, only partially successful dramatic experiment.

The publisher is grateful to many persons who helped in the preparation of this volume. Those who have made suggestions to the translators and to us, suggestions that are often incorporated in these translations, are so numerous that they cannot be listed here. However I would like to single out particularly the contributions of Mildred Adams, Eric Bentley, Rosamond Gilder, the late Angél del Río, Griselda Ohannessian, Lucienne Schupf, Edwin Honig, and May Swenson. Those who helped establish the music for the songs, by calling on their memories and singing the songs in Spanish, are mentioned in a brief Introduction to this music.

The publisher is particularly indebted to Mr. Wolfgang Sauerlander, who has contributed unstintingly in helping to edit the texts and the music, and to Professor Francisco García Lorca, who has been over the translations many times and has brought to them not only his special knowledge of the popular dialects from which some of the author's language and allusions stem but also his remarkably objective familiarity with his brother's mind and work.

R.M.M.

CONTENTS

INTRODUCTION

Alongside *Three Tragedies* which is already published, this volume of comedies and tragi-comedies clearly shows the diversity of the theatre of Federico García Lorca. It is a diversity that extends from a poetic farce like *The Billy-Club Puppets (Los Títeres de Cachiporra)* to the schematic and highly-realistic tragedy of *The House of Bernarda Alba*.

Not only did García Lorca's range include the extremes of dramatic expression, but he tended to combine them in the same play—tragedy and farce, for instance. In this respect *The Love of Don Perlimplín* is very representative of him as a playwright. On the one hand he cultivated the art of short dialogues that are little more than sketches and on the other of such fully developed dramas of character as *Doña Rosita, The Spinster,* which is represented in this volume.

These stark theatre forms practiced by Lorca are strikingly parallel to the forms his poetry took. This fact contradicts the notion that he was primarily a lyric poet who set out consciously to adapt his work to the theatrical medium, as may be the case with other modern poet-playwrights. In the introduction to *Three Tragedies of Lorca* it is shown that Federico's first dramatic attempts coincided with his first poems. With early childhood savings, from his broken-open pottery bank, he bought a toy theatre, and because there were no plays for it, nor for the toy marionettes the family had, he invented plays for it. Many of his childhood games were theatrical in nature. He dressed his brother and sisters and the servants in the Granada house in the clothes of absent grownups, or in towels to become Moors, and they recited dramatic poems or acted out folk ballads he adapted into plays. In these games fiction took on reality, and by the same means reality took on a magical mystery. Later this transformation persisted, and thus, in Lorca, plays resulted from a vision of life which saw everything in dramatic terms. The same vision is often present in his poetry.

This is not the place to try to deal with the motivation of Federico García Lorca, the artist, or to try to evaluate his work. Rather we shall hope to point to some of the roots of his creative process, roots which grew of necessity out of his temperament. There is authenticity in his plays, because they evolved out of personal understanding of the basic elements of theatre as a genre, interwoven with his view of time and space and his vision of life.

Unlike the poets who consciously set out to write for the stage, Federico early developed a language for the theatre nurtured in his dual development as playwright and poet; and this language—his style, in short—unifies the diverse forms he uses and brings together opposing techniques for subtle dramatic purposes. It was because of his diversity that this volume could not be classified simply as "comedies."

THE BILLY-CLUB PUPPETS

After he reached maturity as an artist and a person, Federico García Lorca wrote at least three works for the traditional Spanish puppet theatre and their main character, Don Cristóbal, a kind of Iberian Punch. On January 6, 1923, when he was twenty-four, Federico, with his older friend, the composer Don Manuel de Falla, organized theatricals at the García Lorca house in Granada for his sister Isabel, then a young girl, and her friends. The sixth of January is of course the Feast of the Epiphany, or Twelfth Night, when the Wise Men brought gifts to the Christ-Child. In Spain it is the festival at which children are given gifts.

In the wide doorway between the front parlor and the main living-reception room of the house they set up a stage, and the principal piece of the program was an early thir-teenth-century mystery play of *The Three Wise Men*. The scenery was painted with remarkable skill after illuminations in a medieval mauscript belonging to the University of Granada. The figures, cut out of heavy cardboard, were painted and gilded, and these entered and moved on wooden tracks placed at different levels, manipulated from the sides by Federico himself, his sister Concha, his brother Francisco and other members of the household, who also spoke the lines of the play. The music was chosen and arranged by de Falla from the *Cantigas* of the medieval King Alfonso X (1221-84). There was a three-piece orchestra, comprising a clarinet, a lute and a "harpsichord"—the grand piano "prepared" with brittle paper. All this is described in a copy of the printed program, in the possession of the García Lorca family, which shows that this *piece de resistance* came last.

First on the program was a short *entremés,* or interlude, by Cervantes called *Los dos habladores* (*The Two Chatterboxes*). The *entremés* is a special feature of the Spanish theatre, a comic short play given between the acts of a serious drama, as it was in most of Europe in the Renaissance, but in Spain it took on certain definite characteristics and a special style. As we shall see from the third volume of Lorca's plays planned to be published in English, Federico wrote in this form. Both *The Love of Don Perlimplín* and *The Shoemaker's Prodigious Wife* in the present volume were influenced by qualities of the *entremés,* and it might even be said by those written by Cervantes, who brought to them the same wit and genius to be seen in his major works. In the Twelfth Night theatricals the Cervantes *entremés* was performed by hand puppets. One can imagine that Cervantes would have been pleased by this innovation. He was very fond of puppets, as can be seen in one of the most unforgettable chapters in Part Two of *Don Quixote,* "The Retablo of Maese Pedro," which we should recall was the subject of one of de Falla's musical masterpieces. The musical background for *The Two Chatterboxes* was the *Histoire du Soldat* by Stravinsky, arranged for clarinet, violin and piano, with Don Manuel at the piano.

The second piece on the program was a puppet play written by Federico, *La niña que riega la albahaca* (*The Girl who Waters the Basil Plant*), the manuscript of which has been lost. Federico stated that it was "based on a popular tale," but no one can recall this tale and it is possible he merely wanted to make the play more authentic to his young audience. During it, the small orchestra played music by Albéniz, Debussy and Ravel.

During the changes of the scenery between the three

plays, there appeared in the small puppet proscenium the traditional Don Cristóbal, who addressed himself to his young and delighted audience, calling the children by their first names and carrying on an impromptu dialogue with them, a practice also in the tradition of Spanish hand puppets. Don Cristóbal was manipulated and impersonated by Federico García Lorca so naturally that one could suspect that Federico was animated by the puppet.

Since we do not have the text of *La niña que riega la albahaca,* the first play in this genre in existence is *Los Títeres de Cachiporra,* included in the present volume as *The Billy-Club Puppets.* It is possible that the first version of this play antedated *La niña* because there exists a manuscript dated by Federico August, 1922, some six months earlier than the Epiphany performances. A large part of this 1922 text is incorporated without change in the published text. There was also a version with songs and dances added, which has not been found among Federico's papers.

In *The Billy-Club Puppets* the author has already found a personal dramatic language, and he shows some of the elements that are later to characterize his most famous plays. Here Don Cristóbal is called by his nickname Cristobita and he is the traditional swaggering bully but with many ironic touches invented by Federico. The plot itself, the story of a poor but pretty young girl married off to a presumably rich old monster, is similar to many literary as well as folk plays in Spain, but the author has incorporated his own fantasy, twists of plot, inventions of all sorts. The character "Mosquito" talks directly to the audience. This is also a convention in Spanish popular puppet plays but Federico has written his speeches in a voice that is original and fanciful. In a remarkable way the play shows Federico's ability to integrate popular tradition with poetic sophistication of the most modern sort. There are many intended ambiguities in *The Billy-Club Puppets,* not the least of which is the problem of whether the author intended it to be played by persons acting like puppets, which has been the usual procedure in performances, or by puppets acting like humans. It is clear that the author did not wish this question to be answered.

At a later date, with quite a different approach and technique, Federico García Lorca wrote a much shorter puppet play, the *Retablillo de Don Cristóbal,* a translation of which will appear in the third volume of García Lorca's theatre. We will therefore not discuss this play here, except to say that in it Don Cristóbal is unmistakably a puppet, as in his traditional origins, and that in these three works, all rooted in the author's childhood experiences and memories, the poet revived the puppet tradition which he found in a state close to extinction and raised it to a literary level.

THE SHOEMAKER'S PRODIGIOUS WIFE

This play was first performed in Madrid in 1930 soon after García Lorca had returned from the United States and Cuba. Although it is believed it was first written at an earlier date, he was working on it during his stay in New York. Here also there is more than one known version, in fact several are in the possession of the García Lorca family, and there was likewise a musical version, which was performed later in Argentina. The published text, the one translated in this volume, is considered the best and is thought to be the last. It is true that in these various texts, as in the case of other plays by Lorca that exist in several versions, the differences are not basic and they never affect the structure of the play, but their existence shows the self-exacting methods of the poet and his continual conscious effort toward a goal of perfection. There has often been too much emphasis on his spontaniety and natural gifts. The legend of García Lorca as a divinely-inspired poet was not to his liking, and was only partially true at best.

In this play the author deals with the relation between fantasy and reality and with the essential reality of fantasy. It is a great theme with which Spanish literature, and in fact all Spanish art, has at times concerned itself. It was the main theme of Cervantes, and when García Lorca suggested that there was an echo of Cervantes in *The Shoemaker's Prodigious Wife* one wonders if he was conscious of all that this suggestion implies. To begin with, the plot of the play, again the story of a young woman married to an old man, had been treated by Cervantes in the *entremeses* and in one of *The Exemplary Novels.* But the basic matter of the García Lorca play, fantasy versus reality, is absent from these particular works of Cervantes, which of course also do not have the vivid colors and Andalusian folk quality that characterize *The Shoemaker's Wife.*

The structure of this play and its treatment of characters are reminiscent of the Spanish short play form described briefly above. And of course Cervantes is the great master of this tradition. It can be said that that lively, delightful creature, the "Wife," has literary roots in the ladies in *Court of Divorces,* an interlude by the "creator of the modern novel," but she has her own dramatic development and is created with more tenderness and poetic imagination. Even in the gay, quickly-finished action of the play, she evolves from a light-hearted, young beauty, fretting at her marriage to a diligent, seemingly-dull old man, into a woman of practical wisdom, able to prize the simple virtues of the husband she had driven away.

Here the prologue is not spoken by someone who seems to speak for the author, but by the "Author" himself, and in the play's première Federico played the Author. This Author addresses the audience, half-seriously, half in fun, mocking it and the conventions of the theatre. Shortly, also, he is talking to the protagonist of the play, the "Wife," who is still backstage. He forbids her to enter and start the play, while she, her back to the audience, talks both to him and to characters who are farther offstage, who in fact never really appear. The Author talks to her both as an actress who is to play the part and as a character in the play. With a light touch he is now part of the audience, now addressing it, now part of the backstage preparations, and now involved with the cast and the illusion of the play. Fantasy and reality are immediately blended, and so are the spaces of audience, stage and a world beyond the stage; it is an in-and-out relationship, handled with virtuoso freedom. One is reminded of Federico as the puppet Don

Cristóbal, talking to his sister Isabel and her friends between the plays, at the Twelfth Night performance in 1923. But one is also reminded of the whole gamut of illusion in Spanish art, of such works as *Las Meninas* (*The Ladies-in-Waiting*) by Velasquez.

Indeed this celebrated painting, in the Prado in Madrid, displays in visual terms a very similar attitude. The artist is seen at the left beside his large canvas set up with its back to the spectator. His brush and palette in hand, he is looking out of the picture directly at the space where the spectator stands. The young Infanta, and her ladies-in-waiting, the dwarfs and a dog, are casually amusing themselves at his side, and they pay little attention to the subjects he is painting, who are outside the frame of the picture but who, we learn from their small reflection in a mirror at the back of the room, are King Philip IV and Queen Maria Anna. The picture itself seems to have been eliminated, and the royal couple are an echo of the space in front. In *Don Quixote*, in certain of his *Exemplary Novels* and in some of his plays, Cervantes creates similar illusions, erasing the limits between the reality of the reader and the reality of his characters and their actions, using a rich arsenal of literary devices—which become more than contrivances or tricks—to make the reader see reality in a shifting spectrum.

In *The Shoemaker's Prodigious Wife* and to a different degree in all of García Lorca's work one finds this interplay of levels of reality. The "in-and-out" relationship—of space, time and reality—of the Prologue appears less emphatically in other parts of the play, and is related to the author's mixing of puppets and persons, of realism and poetry, of popular, even "vulgar" speech and refined phrasings, of schematic plots and casual happenings, of violence and sentiment.

DON PERLIMPLÍN

According to a statement of García Lorca this play was already finished in December, 1928. Any performance of it, however, was forbidden during the dictatorship of Primo de Rivera, which continued until 1930, not so much because of the sensual exuberance of Belisa but because the protagonist was an officer of the army and it was considered damaging to military dignity for him to be a cuckold, betrayed by the "five races of the earth." The play was first performed in April, 1933, by the theatrical club "Anfistora" in Madrid.

The Love of Don Perlimplín is also a play of minor proportions, in which a surprising intensity of conflict in the soul of the protagonist and a richness of dramatic elements are combined by the craftsmanship of the author. The cast is reduced to four characters, who interweave their voices in a kind of concerto grosso for four instruments. Maybe none of Lorca's plays shows with more poetic evidence the musical influence in his theatre.

This play also exemplifies how a different treatment of a similar situation can diversify and change totally its meaning. The reader will see that *Perlimplín* is a new version of *The Shoemaker's Wife*. Again there is an old man married to a vital young woman. But now the theme is not only the conflict of fantasy and reality but love is viewed as the conflict of the flesh and the spirit, with the soul triumphant over the body through sacrifice and death.

If in *The Shoemaker's Wife* the author has followed a traditional popular Spanish mode, in *Perlimplín* he has created an atmosphere of refined eroticism. It is an exquisite farce, permeated with a kind of eighteenth-century Italian musicality and sophistication. Against this background Don Perlimplín is one of the most pathetic characters created by Lorca.

DOÑA ROSITA, THE SPINSTER

This play was performed for the first time in 1935 in Barcelona, and it was written not long before *The House of Bernarda Alba*. Of the two, it can be said that this play took longer in ripening, although as usual with García Lorca it was written down in a short time. The poet was slow in conceiving his plays and very rapid in executing them.

Some, like *Blood Wedding,* were written down in less than
a week.

A friend of the author, José Morena Villa, the librarian
of the Royal Palace in Madrid, had read to him from an
Eighteenth Century botany book a description of the *rosa
mutabile,* a variety of rose that opened red, became pale
and then when it wilted and died turned white. The author
said that as soon as his friend had finished reading this
fragment the comedy was completed in his mind. This rose,
of course, figures prominently in the play and is the sad
symbol of Rosita's fate and of the passing of time.

It is a period play, and members of the García Lorca
family remember seeing around their country house near
Granada magazines of the turn-of-the-century, calendars
and small books about the period. With these Federico doc-
umented the play's background, not very thoroughly to tell
the truth, but enough to recreate the atmosphere. It amused
him to bring in some minor historical facts that he must
have gotten from these materials, the purchase by the Shah
of Persia of a twenty-four horsepower Panhard Levasson
motor car, or the death of Count Zbronsky in the Paris-
Madrid auto race. All this is incidental since the action
takes place in a Granada created from the author's early
memories. These also suggested some of the incidents and
characters of the play. It is not surprising that the author
here tried to capture the essence of his native city, its poetic
melancholy and sense of frustration.

The theme of the play is the passage of time. It is a
theme García Lorca had already treated in a more experimental way and from a much different point of view in
If Five Years Pass, which will appear in revised form in the
third volume of García Lorca's theatre. Suffice it to say
here, that this earlier play, dating from 1929 to 1931, the
period of *Poet in New York* and *The Audience,* is possibly
more closely related to the experimental drama of today
than has been supposed.

Several times in *Doña Rosita* the author creates emotions
that are undecided between tears and laughter. This is
true not only of the plight of Rosita, her uncle and aunt

and their house, but of the vistas it gives of provincial middle-class life. These ambiguous emotions are fused, however, by the lyric intensity of the poet and his compassion as a man.

It is a play with abundant social implications; and it is perhaps García Lorca's most conventional work as far as dramatic structure is concerned.

THE BUTTERFLY'S EVIL SPELL

At the end of the volume appears *The Butterfly's Evil Spell,* a comedy of insects, which was given its only production to date in March, 1920, in one of the best theatres in Madrid. The author, almost totally unknown then, was 21 years old. The director of the play was the best qualified at the time, G. Martinez Sierra, author with his wife of *Cradle Song.* Argentinita danced the dance of the Butterfly. The performance was a stentorian failure.

It was not only that a play about beetles or cockroaches, moving about in "modernistic" settings was too much for the taste of a conventional audience, but also that the play itself is not dramatically alive in spite of its tender and ingenious poetry.

On the other hand the play is interesting for what it shows about the author and his development as playwright and poet. Some of the characteristics in his later plays appear timidly in *Butterfly.* It shows how his poetry parallelled his theatre. Anyone who has read García Lorca's first book of poems called simply *Libro de Poemas,* published in 1921, will note the similarity to the poems about animals and insects in that book. Actually the play is a dramatization of one poem that he did not include in the book. It is also interesting to note his early preoccupation with writing for the theatre, at a time after World War I when most poets in their search for "pure poetry" avoided anything to do with the stage.

The last pages of the manuscript of *The Butterfly's Evil Spell* are lacking. This is not surprising—and it is why other manuscripts, as well, are incomplete or missing—for after the murder of Federico García Lorca his papers were avidly sought by the Insurgent authorities in Granada. To avoid seizure these were moved from place to place, and at least once were hidden in a haystack. Those who saw the play have conflicting descriptions of the final action, but all agree that the play ended with the death of the protagonist, Poet Beetle.

It will be noted that in this introduction we have treated the earlier plays in the volume in far greater detail. This was to establish certain basic points, which we hope the reader will find useful.

Francisco García Lorca
August, 1963

THE BILLY-CLUB PUPPETS

(Los Titeres de Cachiporra)

TRAGICOMEDY OF DON CRISTÓBAL
AND MISS ROSITA
A GUIGNOLESQUE FARCE
IN SIX SCENES
AND AN ANNOUNCEMENT

(1922–25)

CHARACTERS

(In order of their appearance)

MOSQUITO

ROSITA

FATHER

COCOLICHE

COACHMAN

DON CRISTOBITA

SERVANT

AN HOUR

YOUNG MEN

SMUGGLERS

QUAKEBOOTS, THE TAVERN KEEPER

CURRITO FROM THE HARBOR

WEARISOME, THE COBBLER

FIGARO, A BARBER

AN URCHIN

A YOUNG LADY IN YELLOW

A BLIND BEGGAR

A BELLE WITH BEAUTY MARKS

AN ACOLYTE

GUESTS WITH TORCHES

FUNERAL PRIESTS

CORTEGE

ANNOUNCEMENT

Two trumpets and a drum sound. Mosquito enters from wherever you wish. Mosquito is a mysterious personage, part ghost, part leprechaun, part insect. He represents the joy of a free life and the wit and poetry of the Andalusian people. He carries a little trumpet of the kind sold at village fairs.

MOSQUITO. Men and women, attention! Son, shut your little mouth, and you, little girl, sit down, by all that's unholy. Now hush so the silence can grow as clear as if it were in its own spring. Hush so the dregs of the last whispers can settle down.

A drum sounds.

My company and I have just come from the theater of the bourgeoisie, the theater of the counts and the marquises, a gold and crystal theater where the men go to fall asleep and the women to fall asleep too. My company and I were prisoners there! You can't imagine how unhappy we were. But one day, through the keyhole, I saw a star twinkling like a little fresh violet of light all aglow. I opened my eye as wide as I could (the wind kept trying to close it with its finger for me) and there, under the star, and furrowed by slow ships, a wide river smiled. Then I, ha! ha! ha!, told my friends about it, and we ran away over the fields, looking for the plain people, to show them the things, the little things, and the littlest little things of this world, under the green mountain moon and the rosy sea-shore moon. We're just as much at home at the midday's daylight as at the midnight's night light. Now the moon is rising and the fireflies slip slowly away to their little grottoes, and the great performance entitled "Tragicomedy of Don Cristóbal and Miss Rosita" is about to begin. Be ready to put up with the mean temper of that little fist shaker Cristóbal, and to weep over the sad lot of Miss Rosita, who, more than she is a woman, is a cold little bird on the pond, a delicate she-bird of the snows. Let's begin!

Exits, but returns running.

And now, wind! Fan all these astonished faces, carry every sigh high above the mountaintops and dry those fresh tears in the eyes of the young ladies who have no sweethearts.

Music.

> Four little leaves were growing
> on my small tree,
> and the wind set them blowing.

SCENE 1

A downstairs room in Doña Rosita's house. Upstage, a large window with a wrought-iron grating, and a door. Through the window, a little orange grove is seen. Rosita wears a rose-colored dress with a bustle, trimmed with ribbons and laces. When the curtain rises, she is sitting at a large frame, embroidering.

ROSITA, *counting the stitches.* One, two, three, four.

She pricks herself.

Ouch!

She puts her finger to her mouth.

Four times I've pricked myself on the final *r* of "To My Adored Father." It's certainly true that needlepoint embroidery is hard work. One, two . . .

She leaves the needle sticking in the canvas.

Oh, how I'd like to get married! I'd dress up with a yellow flower right on my topknot and a veil trailing through the whole street.

She rises.

And when the barber's daughter looked out her window, I'd tell her, "I'm going to get married, and before you do, long before you do, and with bracelets and everything."

Outside, someone whistles.

Oh-ho-ho! It's my boy!

She runs to the window.

FATHER, *offstage*. Rosita-a-a-a!

ROSITA, *frightened*. Wha-a-at?

A louder whistle. She runs and sits at the frame, but blows kisses toward the window.

FATHER, *entering*. I just thought I'd come see if you were doing your embroidery. . . . Work on, my daughter, work on, for that's how we make our living! Oh, how we need the money! Of the five bags full of money we inherited from your uncle, the archpriest, there's not this much left!

ROSITA. What a beard my uncle, the archpriest, had! What an old darling he was!

Whistle outside.

And oh, how he could whistle! How he could whistle!

FATHER. But daughter, what's that you're saying? Have you gone crazy?

ROSITA, *confused*. No, no . . . I made a mistake.

FATHER. Oh, Rosita, how deep in debt we are! What will become of us?

He takes out his handkerchief and weeps.

ROSITA, *weeping*. Well . . . if . . . you . . . I . . .

FATHER. If you'd at least consider getting married, a new day might dawn for us, but I suppose, just now . . .

ROSITA. Why, that's just what I have been considering.

FATHER. Really?

ROSITA. But, hadn't you noticed? How unperspicacious you men are!

FATHER. Well, that suits me to a *T*, to a *T!*

ROSITA. Why, just the thought of an upsweep hairdo and rouge on my cheeks . . .

FATHER. So, you agree, then.

ROSITA, *demure as a nun.* Yes, Father.

FATHER. And you won't change your mind?

ROSITA. No, Father.

FATHER. And you'll always do as I say?

ROSITA. Yes, Father.

FATHER. Well, that's all I wanted to hear.

He starts to leave.

I'm saved from ruin. Saved!

Exits.

ROSITA. What does he mean, "I'm saved from ruin, saved"? Because my sweetheart, Cocoliche, has even less money than we do. Much less! His grandmother left him three coins, a jar of quince preserves, and . . . that's all! Oh, but I love, love, love and double love him!

This is spoken very rapidly.

Dirty old money? That's for the rest of the world. I'll take love.

She runs to the window and waves a large rose-colored 'kerchief through the bars.

COCOLICHE'S VOICE, *singing, accompanied by a guitar.*
> Flying on the breeze
> go the sighs my love is sighing,
> flying on the breeze,
> and on the breezes flying.

ROSITA, *singing.*
> Flying on the breeze
> go the sighs my love is sighing,
> flying on the breeze,
> and on the breezes flying.

COCOLICHE, *appearing at the grating.* Halt, who goes there?

ROSITA, *hiding her face with a large fan and disguising her voice.* A friend.

COCOLICHE. Does perchance a certain Rosita reside in this house?

ROSITA. She's taking the baths.

COCOLICHE, *pretending to leave.* Well, may they do her good.

ROSITA, *uncovering her face.* And would you have had the heart to go?

COCOLICHE. No, I couldn't have.

Sweetly.

At your side my feet become like lead.

ROSITA. You want to know something?

COCOLICHE. What?

ROSITA. Oh, I don't dare!

COCOLICHE. Go on.

ROSITA, *very seriously.* Look, I don't want to be one of those shameless hussies.

COCOLICHE. Well, it seems a very good idea to me.

ROSITA. Look here, it so happens that . . .

COCOLICHE. Say it!

ROSITA. Let me hide behind my fan.

COCOLICHE, *desperate.* Oh, please!

ROSITA, *her face covered.* I'm going to marry you.

COCOLICHE. What? What did you say?

ROSITA. Just what you heard.

COCOLICHE. Oh, Rosita!

ROSITA. And right away . . .

COCOLICHE. Right away I'm going to write to Paris for a baby . . .

ROSITA. Listen, not to Paris. I don't want it to talk like those Frenchmen with their *oui, oui, oui.*

COCOLICHE. Then . . .

ROSITA. We'll write to Madrid.

COCOLICHE. But does your father know of this?

ROSITA. And he's given his permission!

She lowers the fan.

COCOLICHE. Oh, my Rosita! Come here, come. Nearer!

ROSITA. Now, don't get nervous.

COCOLICHE. I feel as if someone were tickling the soles of my feet. Come closer.

ROSITA. No, no; I'll throw you a kiss from here.

They kiss, at a distance. Little bells tinkle.

It always happens! Somebody's coming. Good-by till tonight.

Little bells are heard, and a carriage, drawn by small cardboard horses wearing plumed crests, appears outside the large window grating and stops.

CRISTOBITA, *from the carriage.* No doubt about it, she's the best-looking girl in town.

ROSITA, *spreading out her skirts in a curtsy.* Thank you very much.

CRISTOBITA. I'll take her, definitely. She looks about three feet high. A woman should be just that tall, no more, no less. But what a figure, and what poise! She has almost, almost caught my fancy. Giddap, driver!

Carriage exits slowly.

ROSITA, *mockingly.* Oh, is that so? "I'll take her." What an ugly-looking and bad-mannered gentleman! He must be one of those flirts that come here from other countries.

A pearl necklace flies in through the window.

Oh! What's this? My heavens, what a lovely pearl necklace!

She puts it on and looks at herself in a little hand mirror.

Genevieve of Brabant must have had one just like this when she'd go to the tower of her castle to wait for her husband. And it looks so well on me! But who could have sent it?

FATHER, *entering*. Oh my daughter, joy's complete! Your wedding's all arranged!

ROSITA. How grateful I am to you, and Cocoliche will be so grateful too! Right now . . .

FATHER. Cocoliche? Cocoliche in a pig's eye! What do you mean? I've just given your hand to Don Cristobita, he of the billy-club, who just now came by here in his carriage.

ROSITA. Well, I won't have him, I won't, I won't! And as for my hand, you can't take it away from me. I already have a sweetheart. . . . And I'll throw this necklace away!

FATHER. Well, there's nothing more to be said. This man is very rich, he suits me, and I've made the arrangements because otherwise tomorrow we'd have found ourselves out begging.

ROSITA. I'd rather we begged.

FATHER. I give the orders here because I'm the father. What's done is done and the fat's in the fire. There's no more to be said.

ROSITA. But I . . .

FATHER. Quiet!

ROSITA. As far as I'm . . .

FATHER. Shut up!

Exits.

ROSITA. Oh, oh! So he can dispose of my hand, just like that, and I have to put up with it because the law is on his side.

She weeps.

Why didn't the law stay home where it belongs? If I could only sell my soul to the devil!

Shouting.

Devil, come out; Devil, come out! I refuse to marry that Cristóbal!

FATHER, *entering*. What's all this shouting? Be quiet and get on with your needlework! What's the world coming to? Are children going to tell parents what to do? You're going to obey my every command just as I obeyed my father when he married me to your mother, who, by the bye, had such a moon face that, well . . .

ROSITA. All right then. I'll be quiet!

FATHER, *leaving*. Did you ever see the like?

ROSITA. All right. Between the priest and the papa we girls can only be completely disgusted.

She sits down to embroider.

Every afternoon—three, four—the priest tells us: you are going to Hell yet, you will die from overheat, worse than the dogs. . . . But I say the dogs marry whomever they wish and they fare very well with it. How I would like to be a dog! Because if I pay attention to my father—four, five—I will be in Hell, and if not, I will end up at the other Hell above for not following him. . . . The priests too should shut up and not talk so much . . . because . . .

She dries her tears.

If I don't marry Cocoliche it will be the fault of the priest . . . yes, of the priest . . . to whom, after all, none of this is of the slightest concern. Ay, ay, ay, ay . . .!

CRISTOBITA, *at the window, with his servant*. She's a nice bit. Do you like her?

SERVANT, *trembling*. Yes, sir.

CRISTOBITA. Mouth a trifle too large, but oh, what a tasty dish of a body. . . . I haven't settled the deal yet. . . . I'd like to have a talk with her, but I don't want her to get too familiar. Familiarity is the mother of all vices. Don't you dare contradict me!

SERVANT, *trembling*. But sire!

CRISTOBITA. There are only two ways to deal with people: either never get to know them, or get rid of them!

SERVANT. Merciful heaven!

CRISTOBITA. Listen, you like her!

SERVANT. The best is none too good for Your Grace.

CRISTOBITA. She's a juicy little piece, and she's mine! Mine alone!

Exeunt.

ROSITA. That's all I needed to know. Oh, I'm desperate now. Right away I'll poison myself with potions or with corrosive sublimate.

The wall clock opens and an Hour, dressed in a yellow dress with a bustle, appears.

HOUR, *with her voice and with the bell.* Bong! Rosita, be patient. What can you do? How do you know how things are going to turn out? While it's sunshiny here, it's rainy somewhere else. How do you know what winds will whirl the weather vane on your roof tomorrow? I, since I'm here every day, will remind you of this when you're old and have almost forgotten this moment. Let the water run and the stars go on shining. Rosita, be patient! Bong! One o'clock.

The clock closes.

ROSITA. One o'clock . . . but I'll be damned if I feel like eating!

VOICE, *offstage.*
>   Flying on the breeze
>   go the sighs my love is sighing.

ROSITA. Yes, I see them coming, my lover's sighs.

The wall clock opens once more to reveal the Hour, taking a nap. The bell alone sounds.

ROSITA, *weepily.* The sighs my love is sighing.

CURTAIN

SCENE 2

The little stage represents the plaza of an Andalusian town. To the right, Miss Rosita's house. There should be an enormous palm tree and a bench. Cocoliche comes on from the left, haunting Rosita's neighborhood. He is carrying a guitar, and he wears a little green cloak with black facings. He is dressed in the popular costume of the early nineteenth century. He wears, with an air, a high-brimmed Calaña hat.

COCOLICHE. Not a sign of Rosita. She's afraid of the moon. Moonlight is terribly hard on those who must love in secret.

He whistles.

My whistle has tapped like a little musical pebble against her windowpane. Yesterday she was wearing a black bow in her hair. She said to me: "A black ribbon in my hair is like the blight on a piece of fruit. If you ever see me like this, be sad, for soon the black will go down all the way to my feet." There's something gone wrong with her.

Her balcony, with its row of flower pots, begins to glow with a soft radiance.

ROSITA, *offstage.*

        Oh this vito, vito thrills me,
        and I'll dance it till it kills me. *

COCOLICHE, *going up closer.* Why wouldn't you come out?

ROSITA, *at the balcony, very affectedly and very poetically.* Ah, little lad of mine! This day the Moorish breeze sets all of Andalusia's weather vanes to whirling. One hundred years from now, they'll still be awhirl, and in a similar fashion.

---

* The "vito" is a traditional Andalusian folksong and dance, collected by Federico García Lorca and repopularized by him.

COCOLICHE. What is it you're trying to say?

ROSITA. That you must learn to look on both sides of Time, right and left, and so teach your heart to be resigned.

COCOLICHE. I don't understand you.

ROSITA. It's the next part that's going to be a shock. That's what I'm trying to prepare you for.

Pause, during which Rosita, gasping for breath, sobs comically.

I can't marry you!

COCOLICHE. Rosita!

ROSITA. You're the apple of my eye, but I can't marry you!

She sobs.

COCOLICHE. Are you going to act as balky as a nun now? Have I done anything wrong? Oh, oh, oh!

His weeping is halfway between childish and comic.

ROSITA. You'll find out all about it later. But now, good-by.

COCOLICHE, *shouting and stamping his feet.* Oh, no, no, no, no!

ROSITA. Good-by. Father's calling me.

The balcony shutters close.

COCOLICHE, *to himself.* My ears ring as if I were on top of a mountain. I feel like a paper doll, burning in the flames of my own heart. But I won't have it; no, no, no and no.

Stamping his feet.

What does she mean, she won't marry me? When I brought her that locket from the Mairena fair, she ran her hand over my face. When I gave her the shawl with the roses on it, she looked at me in such a way that . . . and when I brought her the mother-of-pearl fan, the one with Pedro Romero opening his bullfighter's cape on it, she gave me as many kisses as the fan had ribs. Yes, sir! That many kisses! Better if a bolt of lightning had split me in half instead!

He weeps in excellent rhythm.

From the left, various young men dressed in Andalusian costume enter. One of them carries a guitar, another a tambourine. They sing.

> In the River Guadalquivir
> bathes the one whom I would wed.
> My love embroiders 'kerchiefs
> made of silk and colored red.

FIRST LAD. Why, there's Cocoliche.

SECOND LAD. What are you crying about? Get up and don't worry if a bird in the grove hops from one tree to another.

COCOLICHE. Leave me alone!

THIRD LAD. We can't do that. Come on, the wind across the fields will blow your sadness all away.

FIRST LAD. Come on, come on.

They take him with them. Voices, and music. The stage is left empty. The moon shines on the broad plaza. The door of Doña Rosita's house opens and her father appears, dressed in gray, with a pink wig and pink face to match. Don Cristobita enters, dressed in green; he has an enormous belly and a slight hump. He wears a necklace, a bracelet made of little bells, and carries a billy-club that serves him as a walking cane.

CRISTOBITA. So the deal is settled. Agreed?

FATHER. Yes, sir . . . but . . .

CRISTOBITA. But me no buts! The deal is closed. I give you the hundred gold pieces so you can get out of debt and you give me your daughter Rosita . . . and you should be pleased because she's, well, a little . . . overripe.

FATHER. She's sixteen years old.

CRISTOBITA. I said overripe and overripe she is!

FATHER. Yes . . . sir, she is.

CRISTOBITA. But nevertheless, she's a charming girl. What the devil. *Un bocatto di cardinali!*

FATHER, *very seriously.* Does Your Grace speak Italian?

CRISTOBITA. No; as a child I lived in France and Italy, serving a certain Monsieur Pantaloon. . . . But that's none of your affair!

FATHER. No . . . no, sir. . . . Not at all, sir.

CRISTOBITA. So, by tomorrow afternoon I want the blessings all said.

FATHER, *terrified*. But that can't be done, Don Cristobita.

CRISTOBITA. Who's that just said no to me? I don't know why I don't send him to the cliff where I've pushed off so many others. This club you see here has killed a lot of men—French, Italian, Hungarian. . . . I have the list at home. Obey me!—or you'll be dancing to the same tune as the rest of them! It's a long time since this club had something to do and it's ready to jump out of my hands. Be careful!

FATHER. Yes . . . sir.

CRISTOBITA. Now, take the money. Mighty dear she's costing me. Mighty dear! But then, what's done is done. I'm a man who never goes back on his word.

FATHER. (Dear Lord, what kind of a man am I turning my child over to?)

CRISTOBITA. What's that? . . . Come, we'll tell the priest.

FATHER, *trembling*. Very well.

ROSITA, *offstage*.

> Oh this vito, vito thrills me,
> and I'll dance it till it kills me;
> for each moment deep desire
> sets me more and more on fire.

CRISTOBITA. What was that?

FATHER. My little girl singing . . . It's a lovely song!

CRISTOBITA. Bah! I'll give her something to make her voice hoarse—it's more natural!—and to sing that song that goes

> The frog goes croak, croak,
> croak, croak, cr-r-r-oak.

CURTAIN

SCENE 3

*A village tavern. At back, wine barrels and, on the white
walls, blue pitchers. An old bullfight poster and three
oil lamps. Nighttime. The tavern keeper is behind the
counter. He is a man in his shirtsleeves, with bristly hair
and a snub nose. His name is Quakeboots. At right, a
group of classic smugglers, dressed in velvet, bearded,
and carrying blunderbusses. They play cards and sing.*

FIRST SMUGGLER.

> From Cadiz to Gibraltar,
> what a lovely lane!
> The sea knows by my sighing
> I passed that way again.
> Oh, my darling, my darling, oh,
> all those boats in the harbor,
> in the harbor of Málaga!
> From Cadiz to Sevilla,
> so many lemon trees!
> The lemon grove must know me;
> my sighs have stirred the breeze.
> Oh, my darling, my darling, oh,
> all those boats in the harbor of Málaga!

SECOND SMUGGLER. You there! Quakeboots! This blesséd
little song makes me thirsty. Bring some Málaga wine!

QUAKEBOOTS, *lazily*. Right away.

*Through the center door appears a young man dressed
in a full blue cape. He wears a little straight-brimmed
hat. Suspense. He goes on and sits at a table at left,
still without showing his face.*

QUAKEBOOTS. Would Your Grace like something to drink?

YOUNG MAN. Ah, me! No!

QUAKEBOOTS. Have you been around here for some time?

YOUNG MAN. Ah, me! No!

QUAKEBOOTS. It sounds as if you sighed.

YOUNG MAN. Alas! Alas!

FIRST SMUGGLER. Who is he?

QUAKEBOOTS. I can't place him.

SECOND SMUGGLER. You don't suppose he's a . . .

FIRST SMUGGLER. Maybe we'd better be going.

SECOND SMUGGLER. The night is very bright.

FIRST SMUGGLER. And the stars almost touch the rooftops.

SECOND SMUGGLER. At daybreak we'll be in sight of the sea.

Exeunt.

The young man is left alone on the stage. His little head can barely be seen. All the stage is illuminated with a penetrating blue light.

YOUNG MAN. I find the town whiter, much whiter. When I glimpsed it from the mountains, its light went clear through my eyes and right on down to my feet. One day we Andalusians will be whitewashing even our bodies. But on the inside I'm trembling just a little. Oh, Lord! I shouldn't have come.

QUAKEBOOTS. What a state he's in—worse off than Tancred was, but I . . .

Guitars and merry voices sound in the streets. As Quakeboots is leaving.

What's that?

Enter the group of young men with Cocoliche leading them.

COCOLICHE, *drunk.* Quakeboots, give us wine till it comes out of our eyes. Oh, but that will make our tears beautiful; topaz tears, ruby tears . . . Oh, lads, lads!

FIRST LAD. You're so young! We can't let you be sad!

ALL. That's right.

COCOLICHE. She used to say such delicate things to me! She'd say, "Your lips are like two strawberries, not yet quite ripe. . . ."

FIRST LAD, *interrupting him*. She's a very romantic woman, that's all. For that very reason you shouldn't worry. Don Cristobita is fat, drunken, and a sleepyhead who before very long . . .

ALL. Bravo!

SECOND LAD. Who, before very long . . .

Guffaws.

QUAKEBOOTS. Gentlemen, gentlemen.

SECOND LAD. And now for a toast.

FIRST LAD. I drink to what I drink because of drinking is all I think. Cocoliche: at midnight you'll find the door wide open and everything else.

ALL. Olé!

They play the guitars.

SECOND LAD. I drink to Doña Rosita.

YOUNG MAN, *rising*. To Doña Rosita!

SECOND LAD. And may her future husband burst like a balloon!

Laughter.

YOUNG MAN, *going up to them but still concealing his face*. One moment, gentlemen! I'm a stranger here and I'd like to know who this Doña Rosita is to whom you drink so merrily.

COCOLICHE. A stranger and yet so interested?

YOUNG MAN. It could be!

COCOLICHE. Quakeboots, shut the door; even though it's the month of May, this gentleman seems to be very cold.

SECOND LAD. Especially about the face.

YOUNG MAN. I ask you a civil question and you answer with something that's neither here nor there. I think jokes are uncalled for.

COCOLICHE. And just what is it to you who the lady is?

YOUNG MAN. More than you think.

COCOLICHE. Very well, then, the lady is Doña Rosita, who lives there on the plaza, the best singer in Andalusia and my . . . yes! my sweetheart!

SECOND LAD, *coming forward*. And since she's marrying Don Cristobita today, this lad is . . . well, you can imagine!

ALL. Olé! Olé!

Laughter.

YOUNG MAN, *very sadly*. I beg your pardon. I got interested in your talk because I once had a sweetheart who was called Rosita too . . .

SECOND LAD. And now she isn't your sweetheart any more?

YOUNG MAN. No, girls seem to prefer popinjays nowadays. Good night.

He starts to go.

SECOND LAD. Sir, before you leave, I'd like you to drink a glass of wine with us.

He holds out a glass to him.

YOUNG MAN, *at the door, nervously*. Thank you, but I'm not drinking! Good night, gentlemen.

Aside, as he goes.

I don't know how I've been able to hold on to myself.

QUAKEBOOTS. But who the devil was that man, and what did he come here for?

SECOND LAD. Just what I was about to ask you. Who was he, all muffled up in his cape? Why the disguise?

FIRST LAD. You're a poor tavern keeper.

COCOLICHE. It has me worried, worried. . . . That man!

All are uneasy and speak among themselves in low voices.

SECOND LAD, *from the door*. Gentlemen, Don Cristobita is on his way here to the tavern!

COCOLICHE. Now's a good time to knock his face in.

QUAKEBOOTS. I don't want rows in my tavern, so you can just be on your way now.

FIRST LAD. Don't go looking for trouble, Cocoliche! Don't go looking for trouble!

Two lads take Cocoliche out while the others hide behind the tuns. The stage falls silent.

CRISTOBITA, *at the door.* Hr-r-r-r-rmph!

QUAKEBOOTS, *terrified.* Good evening.

CRISTOBITA. You've plenty of wine, haven't you?

QUAKEBOOTS. Any kind you might want.

CRISTOBITA. I want them all, all!

FIRST LAD, *from a corner and in a squeaky voice.* Cristobita.

CRISTOBITA. Eh? Who's that?

QUAKEBOOTS. Some puppy, out in the garden.

CRISTOBITA, *takes his stick and recites.*
> Hide your tail if you're a fox,
> for this club knows where it knocks.

QUAKEBOOTS, *upset.* There's sweet wine . . . white wine . . . sour wine . . . winey wine. . . .

CRISTOBITA. And cheap, eh? You're all a bunch of thieves! Say it, "a bunch of thieves."

QUAKEBOOTS, *trembling.* A bunch of thieves.

CRISTOBITA. Tomorrow I get married to Miss Rosita and I want a lot of wine so I can . . . drink it all myself.

FIRST LAD, *from a barrel.* Cristobita, who drinks and falls asleep!

SECOND LAD, *from another barrel.* Who drinks and falls asleep.

CRISTOBITA. Br-r-r-r. Br, Br, Br! Do your vats talk, or are you trying to joke with me?

QUAKEBOOTS. Who, me?

CRISTOBITA. Smell the club! What does it smell like?

QUAKEBOOTS. Why, it smells . . . like . . .

CRISTOBITA. Say it!

QUAKEBOOTS. Why, like brains!

CRISTOBITA. What did you think?

Furiously.

And about that drinking and sleeping, we'll see who drinks or sleeps, you or me.

QUAKEBOOTS. But Don Cristóbal, but Don Cristóbal.

SECOND LAD, *from a vat.*

> Cristobelly,
> old pot belly!

FIRST LAD. Potbelly!

CRISTOBITA, *with his club.* Your hour has come, rascal, rascal, scoundrel!

QUAKEBOOTS. Oh, Don Cristobita, my friend so dear!

SECOND LAD. Potbelly!

CRISTOBITA. Make fun of me, will you? We'll see about that. Take that, belly; take that, belly!

Exeunt, Don Cristobita whacking him with the club and Quakeboots screeching like a rat. The lads roar with laughter from the vats. Music.

CURTAIN

SCENE 4

The same plaza as before but with the moon shining not nearly as brightly. The yellow palm tree stands out against a blue, starless sky. Two lads enter, Left, tipsy, bringing Cocoliche, drunk also.

FIRST LAD. That blessed Don Cristobita has a nasty temper.

SECOND LAD. What a beating he gave that poor tavern keeper.

FIRST LAD. Say, what're we going to do with this one?

SECOND LAD. Leave him here, and don't worry; he'll wake up when the dew hits his face.

Exeunt.

A flute is heard, coming nearer rapidly, and Mosquito appears. The light grows brighter. Seeing the sleeping Cocoliche, he goes up near to him and blows his little trumpet in one ear. Cocoliche slaps at it and Mosquito backs away.

MOSQUITO. He doesn't know what's happening—of course! —he's a child. But the situation is that Miss Rosita's heart, a heart this tiny, is about to be lost by him.

He laughs.

Miss Rosita's soul is like those little mother-of-pearl boats they sell at fairs, little boats from Valencia fitted out with a pair of scissors and a thimble. Now he'll write "Souvenir" on its stiff sail and go on trudging, trudging. . . .

Exits, playing his little trumpet, and the stage is dark once more.

Enter, the cloaked young man and a village lad.

YOUNG MAN. I'm glad, now, that I came, but I'm so angry I can hardly speak. You say she's getting married?

LAD. Tomorrow, to a certain Don Cristobita, a rich, lazy old man, such a brute that even his shadow breaks things. But I think she's forgotten you by now.

YOUNG MAN. Impossible; she loved me so much, and that was only . . .

LAD. Five years ago.

YOUNG MAN. You're right.

LAD. Why did you leave her?

YOUNG MAN. I don't know. I used to get so tired here. Going down to the harbor, coming back from the harbor. . . . You know! I used to think that the world was a place where bells were always ringing, and that white inns stood along the roads with blonde serving maids in them, wearing their sleeves rolled up to their elbows. But there's nothing like that! It's so dull!

LAD. So what do you plan to do?

YOUNG MAN. I want to see her.

LAD. That's impossible. You don't know Don Cristobita.

YOUNG MAN. Well, I want to see her, cost what it may.

Enter, Right, Wearisome.

LAD. Ah! Here's someone who can help us; it's Wearisome, the cobbler.

Calling.

Wearisome!

WEARISOME. What . . . what . . . what?

LAD. Look, you're going to be very helpful to this gentleman.

WEARISOME. To who . . . to . . . who?

YOUNG MAN, *uncovering his face.* Look at me!

WEARISOME. Currito!

CURRITO. Yes, Currito from the harbor.

WEARISOME, *whacking him on the belly with his hand.* Why, you little scoundrel, how fat you've got.

LAD. Isn't it true that tomorrow you're going to Miss Rosita's to try her bridal shoes on her?

WEARISOME. Yes, . . . yes, . . . yes.

LAD. Then you'll have to let this man go in your place.

WEARISOME. No, no; I don't want to get into any trouble.

CURRITO. But if you knew how well I'd pay you. Come on, now, for your children's sake, I ask you to let me go.

LAD. What's more, he *will* pay you well. He's got money.

CURRITO. Remember, Wearisome,

Pretending to cry.

how much my father loved you.

WEARISOME. Hush! What can I do? I'll let you go! I'll stay home. And it's true . . .

He brings out a large hempen handkerchief.

your father really did love me, very, very much.

CURRITO, *embracing him.* Thank you, many thanks!

WEARISOME. Are you going back to peddling oranges? You used to call out your wares in such a fine way: "O-ranges! O-ranges!"

They go out.

Moonlight begins to flood the stage and the music of guitars runs through it.

COCOLICHE, *talking in his sleep.* Cristobita will beat you, my love. Cristobita has a green belly and a green hump. At night he won't let you sleep with his snorting. And I would have given you so many kisses! How sad, when I saw you with the black ribbon in your hair. . . . "The black will go down to my toes."

The melody of the vito fills the stage. Left, an apparition from Cocoliche's dream appears. It is Doña Rosita, dressed in dark blue, with a wreath of spikenards on her hair and a silver dagger in her hand.

VISION OF ROSITA, *singing.*
>   With this vito, vito, vito,
>   with this vito that I hum you . . .
>   Every hour, oh, my darling,
>   I go farther, farther from you.

The yellow palm tree fills with little silver lights and everything takes on a theatrical blue tinge.

COCOLICHE. Holy Virgin!

He jumps up, but in that moment everything vanishes.

I'm awake; there's no doubt about it, I'm awake. It was she . . . dressed in mourning. I can still almost see her before my eyes . . . and that music . . .

Now, from the balcony, Rosita's voice can really be heard; she is singing, unable to sleep.

ROSITA.

> Oh this vito, vito thrills me,
> · and I'll dance it till it kills me . . .
> for each moment deep desire
> sets me more and more on fire.

COCOLICHE. This is the first time I've ever really wept! I swear it. The first time!

CURTAIN

SCENE 5

An Andalusian street with whitewashed houses. The first house is a cobbler's, the second, a barber's with his armchair and mirror out in the street. Farther down, a great doorway with this sign: "Inn of All the Disillusioned Lovers of the World." Drawn on its door is a huge heart pierced by seven daggers. Morning. Wearisome, in his cobbler's shop, is seated at his bench, sewing on a riding boot. Waiting at his chair is Figaro, dressed in green, wearing a black hair net and curls at his temples, and sharpening a razor on a long strop.

FIGARO. Today's the day I'm expecting the great visit.

WEARISOME. Who's co . . .? Who's com . . .?

A flute backstage finishes out the words.

FIGARO. Don Cristobita's coming; Don Cristobita, the one with the club.

WEARISOME. Don't you thi . . .? Don't you thi . . .?

A little flute finishes out the phrase.

FIGARO. Yes, yes! Of course!

He laughs.

AN URCHIN.
>Shoemaker-aker, thread your thread,
>thread it through the needle's head!

FIGARO. Ah! You great rascal! You rascal!

He runs out in pursuit.

Enter, Currito from the harbor, from the opposite side. He is, as usual, muffled in his cloak. At the center of the stage, he bumps into Figaro, who has turned around rapidly and is coming back.

CURRITO. If you stick me with that razor I'll gouge your eyes out.

FIGARO. Pardon, M'sieu; are you in need of a shave? My barber shop . . .

A piccolo goes on while Figaro eulogizes his own talents in pantomime.

CURRITO. Go to the devil!

FIGARO, *mimicking Currito's call.* O-ranges! O-ranges!

He whistles.

CURRITO, *arriving at the cobbler's.* Wearisome, give me the little boots and the box.

WEARISOME. But . . . but . . . but . . .

He trembles.

CURRITO, *furiously.* Give them to me, I said!

WEARISOME. Take them . . . take them. . . .

FIGARO, *capering.*
>A-pushing and pulling
>my thimble was gone. . . .
>A-pushing and pulling
>I put it back on.

CURRITO, *caressing a pair of rose-colored boots.*
>Oh, little boots
>of Doña Rosita!
>To have the legs in them
>would be much sweeter!

WEARISOME. Now leave me alone! Oh, get away from me!

He goes on plying his awl.

CURRITO, *full of excitement over his boots.* They're like two little wineglasses, two nuns' pincushions, two little sighs.

FIGARO. Something's going on! Without a doubt something's going on! The town reeks of news. Ah, news! but it'll come to my barber shop.

CURRITO, *leaving, with the boots in his hand.* Can it be you're no longer mine, Rosita?

He kisses the boots.

They're like two tears of an early evening's moon, like two little towers in elfland . . . like two . . .

A big kiss.

like two . . .

Exits.

FIGARO. I'll find out what's going on. News can't reach the world till it's first been classified at the barber's. Barber shops are the clearing houses for news. This razor you see here helps break the shell on any secret. We barbers have a scent keener than that of a bulldog; we have a nose for dark words and mysterious gestures. And why not? We're the Lords Mayor of the pate, and, by dint of combing little roads through the forests of hair, we find out what thoughts are going on inside. What tales I could tell about the Sleepers Ugly of the barber's chair!

CRISTOBITA, *entering.* I want a shave right now, yes, sir, right now because I'm going to get married! And I'm not inviting any of you because you're all of you a band of thieves.

Wearisome closes his shop and shows his head through the little window.

FIGARO. They are!

CRISTOBITA, *grabbing up his club.* You are!

FIGARO. They are . . .

Very affirmatively.

pointing to ten o'clock.

He puts away his watch.

CRISTOBITA. Ten or eleven, I want a shave this minute.

WEARISOME. What a little villain he is!

CRISTOBITA, *hitting Wearisome on the head with his club.* Slam, bam, slam!

Wearisome, squeaking like a rat, pulls his head back in.

CRISTOBITA. Let's go!

He sits down.

FIGARO. What a very beautiful head you have! But really magnificent! A very model of heads.

CRISTOBITA. Start shaving!

FIGARO, *lathering.* Trala, la, la!

CRISTOBITA. If you nick me, I'll split you in two. I said in two, and in two it'll be!

FIGARO. Admirable, Excellency! I'm charmed. Tra, lala, lala!

The door of the inn opens and a young lady appears; she is dressed in yellow with a scarlet rose in her hair. An old beggar with an accordion takes a seat at the inn's door.

YOUNG LADY, *singing and playing the castanets.*

>   Oh, I have set my eyes
>   on a boy of talent,
>   tall, dark and slim of waist;
>   he's a likely gallant.
>   With the rose,
>   and the pretty rose,
>   and the olive's green shade . . .
>   Combing her sunlit hair,
>   sits the pretty maid.

ALL.

>   With the rose,
>   and the pretty rose,
>   and the olive's green shade . . .
>   and a-combing her sunlit hair
>   sits the little maid.

YOUNG LADY.

> There in the olive groves,
> maiden, wait and be mine;
> I'll bring you homemade bread
> and a jug of wine.
> With the rose,
> and the pretty rose,
> and the olive's green shade . . .
> and a-combing her sunlit hair
> sits the little maid.

ALL.

> With the rose,
> and the pretty rose,
> and the olive's green shade . . .
> and a-combing her sunlit hair
> sits the little maid.

FIGARO, *looking at the girl*. With the rose, what a pretty rose! Ha, ha, ha! Wearisome, come out here quickly!

The girl stands looking at the sleeping Cristobita in great surprise.

CRISTOBITA, *snoring*. Bz-z-z-z, bz-z-z-z . . .

WEARISOME, *frightened*. No, I don't want to come out.

He is sticking his head out the little window.

FIGARO. This is amazing! Just what I suspected. Really, how stupendous! Don Cristobita has a wooden head. Poplarwood! Ha, ha, ha!

The girl goes up nearer.

And look, look, what a lot of paint . . . what a lot of paint! Ha, ha, ha!

WEARISOME, *coming out*. You'll wake him up!

FIGARO. He has two knots on his forehead. He probably sweats out the rosin there. This was the news! The great news!

CRISTOBITA, *moving*. Hurry up, br-r-r-r, hurry up.

FIGARO. Excellency! Yes, yes . . .

YOUNG LADY.

>   Oh, I have set my eyes
>   on a boy of talent,
>   tall, dark and slim of waist;
>   he's a likely gallant.
>   With the rose,
>   and the pretty rose,
>   and the olive's green shade,
>   and a-combing her sunlit hair
>   sits the little maid.

ALL, *around the sleeping Cristobita, but pianissimo so he won't hear them, but making fun of him.*

>   With the rose,
>   and the pretty rose,
>   and the olive's green shade,
>   and a-combing her sunlit hair
>   sits the little maid.

A belle with beauty patches on her face looks out the window of the inn. She opens and closes a fan.

CURTAIN

SCENE 6

Doña Rosita's house. Facing the audience, two large wardrobes with shutters at the tops of the doors. An oil-burning lamp hangs from the ceiling. The walls are lightly brushed in a pink sugar tone. Over the door, a painting of Saint Rose of Lima under an arch of lemons. Doña Rosita wears a rose-colored dress—a bridal gown full of flounces and most complicated bands. On her throat, a jet necklace.

ROSITA. All is lost! All! I go to the scaffold just like Marianita Pineda. She wore an iron necklace for her marriage to death and I'll wear a necklace . . . yes, a necklace of Don Cristobita's.

She weeps while she sings.

> The speckledy bird was a-sitting,
> sitting on the green lemon tree. . . .

She chokes.

> With her beak and her tail she stirred the leaves
> and blossoms so anxiously.
>   When? Oh, when
> my love shall I see?

Outside a song is heard.

VOICE.

> Rosita, Rosita, to look at your toe,
> if this were allowed me,
> how far would I go?

ROSITA. Oh, Santa Rosa mine! Whose voice is that?

CURRITO, *wrapped in his cloak, he appears suddenly at the door.* May one come in?

ROSITA, *frightened.* Who are you?

CURRITO. A man among men.

ROSITA. But, you have a face?

CURRITO. Very well known to those eyes.

ROSITA. That voice . . .!

CURRITO, *throwing open his cape.* Look at me!

ROSITA, *terrified.* Currito!

CURRITO. Yes, Currito—he who went out into the world but returns now to claim you in marriage.

ROSITA. No, no! Oh, good Lord, go away! I'm engaged now, and besides I don't love you; you left me once. I love Cristobita now. Go away, go away!

CURRITO. I won't go! What do you think I'm here for?

ROSITA. Oh! How unhappy I am! I have a little watch and a mirror of silver but even so, how unhappy I am!

CURRITO. Come away with me. I look at you and I go mad with jealousy.

ROSITA. You're trying to ruin me, you villain!

CURRITO, *trying to embrace her*. My Rosita!

ROSITA. People are coming! Go away, you criminal! Right now!

FATHER, *entering*. What's the matter?

CURRITO. I came to try on Miss Rosita's wedding shoes, because Wearisome couldn't come. They're precious. Worthy of the princesses at the palace.

FATHER. Try them on her!

Doña Rosita sits on a chair. Currito kneels at her feet, and the Father reads a newspaper.

CURRITO. Oh, lilylike leg!

ROSITA, *in a low voice*. Villain!

CURRITO, *loudly*. Raise your skirts a little.

ROSITA. There.

Currito puts one of the boots on her foot.

CURRITO. Let's see—a little bit higher?

ROSITA. That's enough, shoemaker.

CURRITO. A little bit higher!

FATHER, *from his chair*. Do as he says, child; a little higher.

ROSITA. Oh!

CURRITO. A little bit higher!

He stares at Rosita's leg.

A little bit higher!

FATHER. I'm going now. The boots are lovely. . . . And on the way I'll close this door. It's a little chilly.

As he tries to close the center door.

Certainly hard to close. Must be the dampness.

CURRITO.

> Oh what lovely toes
> Your Grace has wherever she goes!
> Oh what lovely,
> what lovely toes!

ROSITA, *rising*. Evil man, dog of a Jew!

CURRITO. Rose. Little Rose of the Maytime.

ROSITA, *screeching pianissimo*. Oh, oh, oh!

She runs about the stage.

Don Cristobita is coming! Run out this way!

They find the door locked.

Oh, did Father lock this door?

CURRITO, *trembling*. The truth of the matter is that . . .

ROSITA. I can hear his footsteps on the stairs! Oh, Saint Rose inspire me!

Meanwhile Currito is trying to open the door.

Ah! . . . Come here!

She opens the right corner wardrobe and hides him there.

That's it! Oh, I thought I'd die.

CRISTOBITA, *offstage*. Br-r-r-r-r!

ROSITA, *singing and half crying*.

> The speckledy bird was a-sitting,
> sitting on the green lemon tree. . . .
> > When? Oh, when
> > my love shall I see?

She chokes.

CRISTOBITA, *at the door*.

> I smell a human
> on which to sup.
> If I can't have him,
> I'll eat *you* up.

ROSITA. What won't you think up next, Cristobita!

CRISTOBITA. I don't want you talking with anybody. Anybody! I've warned you! (Oh, how tasty she is! What a pair of little hams she has!)

ROSITA. I, Cristobita . . .

CRISTOBITA. We're getting married right away. . . . And listen! You've never seen me kill anybody with the stick? No? Well, you will. I go, wham! wham! wham! . . . and over the cliff.

ROSITA. Yes, that's very nice.

ACOLYTE, *through the window.* The Holy Father wants me to tell you you can come whenever you're ready now.

CRISTOBITA. We're coming! Olé, olé, we're coming!

He picks up a bottle and dances while he drinks.

ROSITA. Well, then . . . I'll go put on my veil.

CRISTOBITA. I'm going too: I'll put on a huge hat and tie ribbons on my club. I'll be right back.

He goes off dancing.

CURRITO, *looking out through the wardrobe shutters.* Open the door.

Rosita starts toward the wardrobe but just at that moment Cocoliche enters through the window with a great leap.

ROSITA. Oh!

She runs to him and throws herself in his arms.

Nobody! In all the world I don't love anybody but you.

Cocoliche takes her in his arms.

COCOLICHE. Darling!

CURRITO, *from the wardrobe.* I suspected as much! You're a fallen woman.

COCOLICHE. What does this mean?

ROSITA. I'm going crazy!

COCOLICHE. What are you doing in that rat hole? Come out in the open like a man!

He beats on the wardrobe.

ROSITA. Have pity on me!

COCOLICHE. Pity on you? Oh, despicable strumpet!

CURRITO. I'd like to strangle both of you.

COCOLICHE. Come out of there! Break the doors down! Coward!

ROSITA. Cristobita is coming! Have pity, Cristobita is coming!

CURRITO. O-o-o-pen!

COCOLICHE. Let him come! Then he'll see how his fiancée makes arrangements with her lover.

ROSITA. I'll explain to you later, my love. Run!

CRISTOBITA, *offstage.* Rosita . . . little one!

ROSITA. It's too late. Here!

She opens the other wardrobe and hides Cocoliche; then she throws a pink veil over her head.

I'm dying!

She tries to pretend to sing.

CRISTOBITA, *entering.* What was that noise?

ROSITA. It was . . . the guests, waiting at the door.

CRISTOBITA. I don't want any guests!

ROSITA. Well . . . they're here!

CRISTOBITA. Well, if they're here, let them go away. Let them go away!

Aside.

And I mean to find out about that noise.

Aloud.

Come, Rosita. Eh? Oh, how tasty she is!

The center door opens and the wedding guests are seen. They carry large hoops decorated with colored paper roses under which Rosita and Don Cristobita pass.

FIRST GUEST. Long live the bride and groom!

ALL. Long may they live!

Music.

The heads of Currito and Cocoliche peek out through the shutters.

CURRITO. I'm going to explode!

COCOLICHE. So you're the lover of that creature? I'll meet you face to face later!

CURRITO. Whenever you say, stupid!

COCOLICHE. If this wardrobe weren't made of iron . . .

CURRITO. Ha!

COCOLICHE. I'd gladly take your nose off with a single bite!

Outside may be heard a "Long live the bride and groom! Long may they live!"

The ceremony is about to start . . . she's forgetting me forever!

He weeps.

CURRITO, *theatrically.* I returned to this town to learn how to forget.

COCOLICHE. Never again will she call me "Little Fruit Face" . . . nor I call her "Little Almond Face." . . .

CURRITO. I shall depart forever, forever!

COCOLICHE. Boo, hoo, hoo!

CURRITO. Ingrate, ingrate, ingrate!

Outside, church bells, fireworks and music can be heard.

COCOLICHE. I won't be able to go on living!

CURRITO. I'll never be able to look at another woman!

The two puppets weep.

MOSQUITO, *entering, Left.* There's no need to weep, little friends, there's no need. The earth is full of little white roads, smooth little roads, foolish little roads. . . . Ah, but lads, why spill away such pearls? You aren't princes. After all . . . the moon is not so much on the wane, and the breezes neither come nor go. . . .

He sounds his little trumpet and goes.

They neither come nor go. Neither come nor go . . .

Cocoliche and Currito heave a deep sigh and stand staring at each other.

The central door opens suddenly and the wedding cortege appears. Don Cristóbal and Miss Rosita bid them good-by at the door and close it. There are music and the tolling of bells in the distance.

CRISTOBITA. Oh, Rosita of my heart! Oh, Rosita!

ROSITA. He'll probably kill me now with the club.

CRISTOBITA. Are you sick? I thought you sighed! But that's because I please you so. I'm old and I understand things. Look what a suit I'm wearing! And what boots! Trala-la-la! Ah, bring sweets and wine, lots of wine!

Enter, a servant with some bottles. Cristobita takes one and begins to drink.

Ah, pretty Rosita! Tiny thing! Little almond! Isn't it true that I'm very beautiful? I'll give you a kiss! Here! Here!

He kisses her. At this moment Cocoliche and Currito look out of the shutters and let out a scream of rage.

What's that? Could it be that this house is haunted?

He takes up the club.

ROSITA. No, no, Cristóbal! It's the termites! It's the children out in the street! . . .

CRISTOBITA, *putting down the club.* They make a lot of noise, *caramba!* They make a lot of noise!

ROSITA, *hiding her terror.* When are you going to tell me the stories you promised me?

CRISTOBITA. Ha, ha, ha! They're very pretty, pretty as that poppy-face of yours.

He drinks.

The story of Don Tancredo, mounted on his pedestal. You know it? Ho-o-o-o! And the story of Don Juan Tenorio, Don Tancredo's cousin, and my cousin too. Yes sir! My cousin! You say it: "My cousin!"

ROSITA. Your cousin!

CRISTOBITA. Rosa! Rosa! Tell me something!

ROSITA. I love you, Cristobita.

CRISTOBITA. Olé, olé!

He kisses her. There is another scream that issues from the wardrobes.

I'll put a stop to this, a stop and a definite end! Br-r-r-r-r!

ROSITA. Oh! No, don't get angry.

CRISTOBITA, *with the stick.* Whoever is in there, come out!

ROSITA. Look, don't be angry. A bird just flew past the window, with wings . . . this big!

CRISTOBITA, *imitating her*. This big! This big! You think I'm blind?

ROSITA. You don't love me! . . .

She weeps.

CRISTOBITA, *softened*. Shall I believe you . . . or shall I not believe you?

He sets his club down.

ROSITA, *affectedly poetic*. What a clear little night dwells now upon the rooftops. At this hour, children count the stars and old men fall asleep in the saddle.

Cristobita sits down, places his feet on the table and starts to drink.

CRISTOBITA. I'd like to be made all of wine and drink myself up. Ho-o-o-o! And my belly to be a cake, a great curly cake with sugar plums and sweet potatoes . . .

Cocoliche and Currito look out from the wardrobes and sigh.

Who's that sighing?

ROSITA. I . . . It was I, thinking of when I was a little girl.

CRISTOBITA. When I was a boy they gave me a cake bigger than the moon and I ate it all by myself. Ho-o-o! All by myself.

ROSITA, *romantically*. The mountains of Cordoba have shadows under their olive groves, trampled shadows, dead shadows, that never move. Oh, to be under their roots. The mountains of Granada have feet of light and snowy headdresses. Oh, to be under their springs! Seville has no mountains.

CRISTOBITA. It has no mountains, no . . .

ROSITA. Long roads, colored orange. Oh, to lose one's self along them!

Cristobita, listening to her, much as a person listening to a violinist, has fallen asleep with a bottle in his hand.

CURRITO, *very softly.* Open the door!

COCOLICHE. Don't open mine! I want to die here.

ROSITA. Be still, for heaven's sake!

Enter, Mosquito, who begins to blow his trumpet around Cristobita. The latter slaps at him.

CURRITO. I'll go where you'll never see me again.

ROSITA. I never loved you. You're a wanderer.

COCOLICHE. What's this I hear?

ROSITA. You're the only one I love, my love!

COCOLICHE. Ah, but you're already married!

CRISTOBITA. Br-r-r-r . . . Pesky mosquitoes! Pesky mosquitoes!

ROSITA. Santa Rosa, don't let him wake up!

She goes toward one wardrobe and very carefully opens it.

All of this scene should be played very quickly, but in low voices.

CURRITO, *coming out of the wardrobe.* Farewell forever, O ingrate! My one regret is that I'll never forget you.

At this moment Mosquito strikes Cristobita a sharp blow on the head with the trumpet and wakes him up.

CRISTOBITA. Ah! What? What? This is unbearable! Br-r-r-r!

CURRITO, *bringing out a dagger.* Patience, my dear sir, patience!

CRISTOBITA. I'll kill you, I'll run you through a grinder, I'll pulverize your bones! You'll pay for this, Miss Rosita, fallen woman! And you cost me a hundred coins! Br-r-r-r! Smash, bing, bang! I'm choking with rage! Bing! Bang! What are you doing there?

CURRITO, *trembling.* What . . . whatever I please.

CRISTOBITA. Ahr-r-r-r! Whatever you please? Well, man! Take this, whatever! Take this, please!

Currito stabs at Cristobita with his dagger but it sticks in the sleepyhead's chest in a strange way. During all

*this, Rosita has been trying to open the center door and
at this moment has succeeded in throwing it wide. Currito flies through it, pursued by Cristobita, who is saying*

Take this, whatever! Take this, please!

*Rosita has been giving vent to piercing screams or laugh-
ing hysterically. During this while, the characters should
be supported by various flutes from a little orchestra.*

COCOLICHE. Let me out of here; I'll kill him when he
comes back!

ROSITA. Let you out?

She goes to open.

No, I won't! Oh!

COCOLICHE. Rosita, let me strangle him.

ROSITA. Shall I?

She goes to open.

No I won't! He's coming now and he'll kill us.

COCOLICHE. That way we'll die together!

ROSITA. Shall I? Oh, yes . . . I'll let you out!

She opens the wardrobe.

My little heart! Little tree out of my garden!

COCOLICHE, *embracing her.* My hothouse carnation! Little
handful of cinnamon!

An idyll, like an opera duet, begins.

ROSITA. Go back to your house; I'll stay here and die.

COCOLICHE. Never, little rose among flowers. There on
that little star I'll make you a swing and a silvery balcony.
From there we'll watch how the world shimmers, dressed
in moonlight.

ROSITA, *forgetful of everything and in great happiness.*
How romantic you are, my darling! I believe I must be a
flower, dropping my petals in your hands.

COCOLICHE. Every day you look rosier to me; every day
you seem to strip off another veil and surge forth naked.

ROSITA, *placing her little head upon her sweetheart's
breast.* Inside your breast a thousand birds have taken

wing; my love, when I look at you, I seem to stand before a little fountain.

Offstage, Cristobita's voice is heard, and Rosita comes out of her ecstasy.

Run!

CRISTOBITA, *appearing at the doorway and standing thunderstruck.* Ahr-r-r-r! You have lovers by the pair! Get ready for the cliff! Bing! Bang! Br-r-r-r!

Cocoliche and Rosita kiss desperately in front of Cristobita.

Unbearable! I'm the one who killed three hundred Englishmen, three hundred Constantinopolitans! I'll give you something to remember me by! Oh! Ouch!

The club falls from his hand and a great grinding of springs is heard.

Oh, my little belly! Oh, my little belly! It's your fault I've burst, I've died! Oh, I'm dying! Oh, tell them to call the priest! Oh!

ROSITA, *screeching piercingly and running about the stage dragging her long train.* Papa-a-a! Papa-a-a!

CRISTOBITA. Ahr-r-r-r! Bang! I'm done for!

He staggers backward with his arms on high and then falls across the footlights.

ROSITA. He's dead! Oh, good heavens, what a compromising situation!

COCOLICHE, *going up to him fearfully.* Say, he doesn't have any blood!

ROSITA. No blood?

COCOLICHE. Look! Look at what's coming out of his belly button! Sawdust!

ROSITA. I'm frightened!

COCOLICHE. You know something?

ROSITA. What?

COCOLICHE, *emphatically.* Cristobita wasn't a real person!

ROSITA. What? Oh, don't even tell me! How disgusting! Wasn't he really a person?

FATHER, *entering*. What is it? What is it?

Enter, various puppets.

COCOLICHE. Look!

FATHER. He's burst!

The center door opens and other puppets appear, carrying torches. They wear red capes and little black hats. Mosquito goes in front, carrying a white banner and playing his trumpet. They bear an enormous coffin on which peppers and radishes are painted, instead of stars. Priests come chanting. A funeral march is played on the flutes.

PRIEST.   *Uri memento.*
               A man is dead.

ALL.
               Dead and gone, dead and gone
               Cristobalón.

A PRIEST.
               Whether we sing or don't
               We earn our five pesetas.

When they pick up Cristobita, he resounds in an amusing manner, like a bassoon. They all step back, and Doña Rosita weeps. They come back to him again and he doesn't sound quite as loudly as before, till finally his sighs are those of a piccolo, whereupon they throw him in the coffin. The cortege marches about the stage to the laments of the music.

COCOLICHE. Now I feel as if my chest were full of jingle bells, full of lots of little hearts. I'm just like a field of flowers.

ROSITA. My tears, my little kisses will all be for you; you're my carnation.

MOSQUITO, *as he leads off the assembly.*
               We're going to bury
               the great bread sack,

Cristobita, the drunkard,
who won't come back.
Ran,
rataplan,
rataplan,
rataplan.
Rataplan!

Cocoliche and Rosita are left, embracing. Symphony.

CURTAIN

THE SHOEMAKER'S PRODIGIOUS WIFE

A VIOLENT FARCE IN TWO ACTS
AND A PROLOGUE

(1930)

CHARACTERS

SHOEMAKER'S WIFE
NEIGHBOR IN RED (Red Neighbor)
NEIGHBOR IN PURPLE (Purple Neighbor)
NEIGHBOR IN GREEN (Green Neighbor)
NEIGHBOR IN BLACK (Black Neighbor)
NEIGHBOR IN YELLOW (Yellow Neighbor)
FIRST OVER-PIOUS WOMAN
SECOND OVER-PIOUS WOMAN
SACRISTAN'S WIFE
THE AUTHOR
THE SHOEMAKER
THE BOY
THE MAYOR
DON BLACKBIRD
YOUTH WITH SASH (Sash Youth)
YOUTH WITH HAT (Hat Youth)
NEIGHBORS, OVER-PIOUS PEOPLE, PRIESTS
   AND VILLAGERS.

PROLOGUE

Gray curtain.

The Author appears. He enters rapidly. He carries a letter in his hand.

THE AUTHOR: Worthy spectators . . .

Pause.

No, not "worthy spectators"; merely "spectators." And not because the author doesn't consider the public worthy—quite the contrary. It's only that behind that word "worthy" there seems to be a slight tremor of fear and a sort of plea that the audience should be generous with the mimicking of the actors and the workmanship of the playwright's genius. The poet does not ask benevolence, but attention, since long ago he leapt that barbed fence of fear that authors have of the theater. Because of this absurd fear, and because the theater on many occasions is run for financial reasons, poetry retires from the stage in search of other surroundings where people will not be shocked at the fact that a tree, for example, should become a puff of smoke, or that three fishes through their love for a hand and a word should be changed into three million fishes to feed the hunger of a multitude. The author has preferred to set the dramatic example in the live rhythm of an ordinary little shoemaker's wife. Everywhere walks and breathes the poetic creature that the author has dressed as a shoemaker's wife with the air of a refrain or a simple ballad, and the audience should not be surprised if she appears violent or takes bitter attitudes because she is ever fighting, fighting with the reality which encircles her and with fantasy when it becomes visible reality.

Shouts of the Shoemaker's Wife are heard: "I want to come out!"

I'm hurrying! Don't be so impatient to come out; you're not going to wear a dress with a long train and matchless plumes; but just a torn dress; do you hear? The dress of a shoemaker's wife.

Voice of the Shoemaker's Wife is heard: "I want to come out!"

Silence!

The curtain is drawn and the darkened stage appears.

Every day in the cities it dawns like this, and the audience forgets its half-world of dreams to go to market just as you enter your house, prodigious little shoemaker's wife.

The light is increasing.

Let's start! You come in from the street.

Voices arguing are heard. To the audience.

Good evening.

He takes off his tall silk hat and it becomes illuminated with a green light from within. The Author tips it over and a gush of water falls from it. The Author looks at the audience a bit embarrassedly, and retires backward, with great irony.

I beg your pardon.

Exit.

ACT ONE

*The Shoemaker's house. Shoemaker's bench and tools.
A completely white room. Large window and door. The
backdrop seen through the large window is a street, also
white with some small doors and windows in gray. To the
right and left, doors. All this scene shall have an air of
optimism and exalted happiness to the smallest details.
The soft orange light of afternoon pervades the scene.*

*When the curtain rises the Shoemaker's Wife enters
furiously from the street and pauses at the door. She is
dressed in angry green, and wears her hair drawn back
tight and adorned with two big roses. She has an aggres-
sive and a sweet air at the same time.*

WIFE. Be quiet, long tongue! Ugly Kate! Because if
I've done it . . . if I've done it—it's because I wanted to.
If you hadn't run into your house I would have dragged
you along, you dusty little snake; and I say this so that
all those who are behind the windows may hear me. For
it's better to be married to an old man than to a one-eyed
one as you are. I don't want any more conversation—not
with you nor with you—nor with any one—nor with any
one!

Enters, slamming door.

I knew that with that kind of people one couldn't talk
even for a second . . . but I'm to blame—I and I . . .
because I ought to stay in my house with . . . I almost
don't want to believe it, with my husband. If anybody had
told me, blonde and dark-eyed—and what a good com-
bination that is, with this body and these colors so very
very beautiful—that I was going to marry a . . . I would
have pulled my hair out.

She weeps. There is a knock at the door.

Who is there?

Another knock at the door. No answer. Furiously.

Who's there?

BOY, *fearfully, outside.* A friend.

WIFE, *opening.* Is it you?

Sweetly and touched.

BOY. Yes, Mrs. Shoemaker. Were you crying?

WIFE. No. It's just that one of those mosquitoes that go ping——ng bit me in the eye.

BOY. Do you want me to blow in it?

WIFE. No, my child, it's gone.

She caresses him.

And what is it you want?

BOY. I brought these patent-leather shoes, which cost five dollars, for your husband to repair. They are my older sister's, the one who has the nice skin and wears two bowknots because she's got two—one for one day and the other for the other—at her waist.

WIFE. Leave them here. They'll be repaired sometime.

BOY. My mother says you must be careful not to hammer them too much because patent leather is very delicate—so the patent leather won't be hurt.

WIFE. Tell your mother my husband knows what he's doing. And that she wishes she knew how to season a good dish with pepper and bay the way my husband knows how to repair shoes.

BOY, *his face puckering.* Don't be angry at me; it's not my fault. And I study my grammar very well every day.

WIFE, *sweetly.* My child! My treasure! I'm not angry at you!

Kisses him.

Take this doll. Do you like it? Well, take it.

BOY. I'll take it because, well—since I know you're not going to have any children. . . .

WIFE. Who told you that?

BOY. My mother was talking about it the other day. She was saying: "The shoemaker's wife won't have any children," and her friend Rafaela and my sisters laughed.

WIFE, *nervously*. Children? Maybe I'll have better-looking ones than all of them—and with more courage and honor—because your mother—I think you ought to know this . . .

BOY. You take the doll. I don't want it!

WIFE, *changing*. No, no—you keep it, son. This has nothing to do with you!

The Shoemaker appears at left. He wears a velvet suit with silver buttons, short trousers and a red tie. He goes toward his bench.

WIFE. May God help you!

BOY, *frightened*. Good health to you! Till I see you again! Congratulations! *Deo Gratias!*

Goes running to the street.

WIFE. Good-by, child. If I had burst before I was born I wouldn't be suffering these trials and tribulations. Oh, money, money! The one who invented you should have been left without hands or eyes.

SHOEMAKER, *at the bench*. Woman, what are you saying?

WIFE. Something that doesn't concern you!

SHOEMAKER. Nothing concerns me. I know I must control myself.

WIFE. I also have to control myself. . . . Just think of it: I'm only eighteen years old.

SHOEMAKER. And I—fifty-three. That's why I hush up and am not angry with you! I know too much! I work for you, and may God's will be done. . . .

WIFE, *her back is to her husband, but she turns and advances tenderly, moved*. Not that, my child. Don't say that!

SHOEMAKER. But, oh, if I were only forty years old, or forty-five even!

Hammers the shoe furiously.

WIFE, *aroused.* Then I would be your servant; isn't that
so? One can't be good. What about me? Am I not worth
anything?

SHOEMAKER. Woman, control yourself.

WIFE. Aren't my freshness and my face worth all the
money in this world?

SHOEMAKER. Woman—the neighbors will hear you!

WIFE. Cursed be the hour, cursed be the hour, when I
listened to my friend Manuel.

SHOEMAKER. Would you like me to make you some
lemonade?

WIFE. Oh, fool, fool, fool!

Strikes her forehead.

With as good suitors as I've had.

SHOEMAKER, *trying to soften her.* That's what people say.

WIFE. People? It's known everywhere. The best in these
parts. But the one I liked best of all of them was Emiliano.
You knew him, Emiliano—the one who used to ride a black
mare covered with tassels and little mirrors, carrying a willow
wand in his hand, with his copper spurs shining. And what
a cape he had for winter! What sweeps of blue broadcloth
and what trimmings of silk!

SHOEMAKER. I had one like that too; they're lovely capes.

WIFE. You? What could you have had? Now why do
you fool yourself? A shoemaker has never in his life worn
such clothes.

SHOEMAKER. But, woman, can't you see? . . .

WIFE, *interrupting him.* And then I had another suitor.

The Shoemaker hammers the shoe furiously.

He was rather young. . . . He was maybe eighteen years
old. That can be said very quickly! Eighteen years!

The Shoemaker twists uncomfortably.

SHOEMAKER. I was eighteen once, too.

WIFE. You never in your life were eighteen years old!
But he was. And such things as he used to say to me.
Look. . . .

SHOEMAKER, *hammering furiously*. Will you be quiet? You're my wife whether you like it or not—and I'm your husband. You were perishing without a dress or a home. Why did you love me? Deceiver! Deceiver! Deceiver!

WIFE, *rising*. Shut up! Don't make me speak more than is wise—and get to your duty. I can hardly believe it!

Two neighbors wearing mantillas cross the window smiling.

Who could have told me, old bag-o'bones, that you would repay me like this? Hit me if you want. Go on, throw the hammer at me!

SHOEMAKER. Oh, woman, don't raise such a row. Look, the people are coming—oh, my God!

The two neighbors cross again.

WIFE. I've gone below my station. Fool, fool, fool! Cursed be my friend Manuel. Cursed be the neighbors. Fool, fool, fool.

Leaves, striking her forehead.

SHOEMAKER, *looking in a mirror, counting his wrinkles*. One, two, three, four . . . and a thousand.

Puts up the mirror.

But it serves me right, yes sir. Because, let's see: why did I marry? I should have known after reading so many novels that men like all women—but women don't like all men. And I was so well off! My sister, my sister is to blame. My sister who kept saying: "You're going to be left alone." You're going to be this and that. And that was my undoing. May lightning strike my sister, may she rest in peace!

Outside, voices are heard.

What could that be?

NEIGHBOR IN RED, *at the window, accompanied by her two daughters dressed in the same color. With great spirit.* Good afternoon!

SHOEMAKER, *scratching his head*. Good afternoon.

RED NEIGHBOR. Tell your wife to come out here. Girls, will you please stop crying! Tell her to come out here and we'll see if she gossips as much to my face as behind my back!

SHOEMAKER. Oh, neighbor of my soul, don't raise a row, by the little nails of Our Lord! What do you want me to do? Understand my situation; all my life fearing marriage . . . because marriage is a very serious thing, and then, finally, what you can see.

RED NEIGHBOR. You poor man! How much better off you would have been if you had married with people of your own kind, these girls, for example, or others of the village.

SHOEMAKER. My home is not a home, it's a madhouse!

RED NEIGHBOR. You tear my soul! As good a name as you've had all your life.

SHOEMAKER, *looking to see if his wife is coming.* Day before yesterday, she carved up the ham that we had saved for Christmas—and we ate it all. Yesterday we ate nothing but egg soup and parsley; well then, because I protested over that, she made me drink three glasses of unboiled milk one right after the other.

RED NEIGHBOR. How brutal!

SHOEMAKER. And so, little neighbor of my heart, I would be grateful to you with my whole soul, if you would leave.

RED NEIGHBOR. Oh, if your sister still lived! Now there was a . . .

SHOEMAKER. You see . . . and on your way you can take these shoes that are ready.

The Shoemaker's Wife looks in at the door on the left where she watches the scene unnoticed from behind the curtain.

RED NEIGHBOR, *ingratiatingly.* How much are you going to charge me for these? Times are always getting harder.

SHOEMAKER. Whatever you want. Whatever isn't too hard on either of us . . .

RED NEIGHBOR, *nudging her daughters with her elbow.* Are two pesetas all right?

SHOEMAKER. I leave that to you!

RED NEIGHBOR. Oh, well, I'll give you one then. . . .

WIFE, *entering furiously.* Thief!

The women squeal and are frightened.

Do you have the face to rob a man this way?

To her husband.

And you to let yourself be robbed? Give me those shoes. Until you give me ten pesetas for them, I'll keep them here.

RED NEIGHBOR. Lizard! Lizard!

WIFE. Be very careful what you're saying!

GIRLS. Oh, let's go, let's go! For heaven's sake!

RED NEIGHBOR. It serves you right, having such a wife! Make the most of it!

They go out quickly. The Shoemaker shuts the door and the window.

SHOEMAKER. Listen to me a moment. . . .

WIFE, *mulling.* Lizard . . . Lizard. What? What? What? . . . What are you going to tell me?

SHOEMAKER. Look, my child: all my life it has been my constant concern to avoid rows.

The Shoemaker is constantly swallowing.

WIFE. Have you got the courage to tell me I cause a row when I come out to defend your interests?

SHOEMAKER. I don't say any more, except that I have fled from rows just as salamanders do from cold water.

WIFE, *quickly.* Salamanders! Oh, how nasty!

SHOEMAKER, *armed with patience.* They have provoked me; they have, at times, even insulted me, and not being even a little bit a coward, I would swallow all that for fear of being the center of attention, and having my name bandied back and forth by gossips and idlers. Therefore, you're warned. Have I spoken clearly? This is my last word.

WIFE. Well, now, let's see. What does all that matter to me? I married you. Isn't your house clean? Aren't you fed? Don't you wear collars and cuffs such as you had never in your life worn before? Don't you carry your watch

—so beautiful with its silver chain and charms—which I wind every night? What more do you want? Because I will be everything except a slave. I'll always do just as I want to.

SHOEMAKER. No need to tell me. We've been married three months. I loving you and you mocking me. Can't you see that I can't stand jokes like that?

WIFE, *seriously, as if dreaming*. Loving me, loving me . . . but

Roughly.

what is that about loving me? What do you mean, "loving me"?

SHOEMAKER. You may think I'm blind, but I'm not. I know what you do and what you don't do; and now I'm fed up with it—to here!

WIFE, *furious*. Well, it's all the same to me whether you're fed up or not. Because you don't matter three whistles. Now you know!

Weeps.

SHOEMAKER. Couldn't you speak a little lower?

WIFE. What you deserve—you're such a fool—is for me to fill the street full of shouting.

SHOEMAKER. Fortunately, I think this will end soon; because I don't know how I have the patience.

WIFE. Today we don't eat here—so you can go somewhere else to look for your food.

The Wife leaves quickly in a fury.

SHOEMAKER, *smiling*. Tomorrow, maybe you will have to look too.

Goes to bench.

Through the central door the Mayor appears. He is dressed in dark blue, wears a large cape, and carries the long staff of his office with silver decorations. He speaks slowly and with great sluggishness.

MAYOR. Working?

SHOEMAKER. Working, Mr. Mayor.

MAYOR. Much money?

SHOEMAKER. Enough.

Shoemaker continues working. The Mayor looks every-where curiously.

MAYOR. Everything's not all right with you.

SHOEMAKER, *without raising his head.* No.

MAYOR. Your wife?

SHOEMAKER, *assenting.* My wife.

MAYOR, *sitting.* That comes of marrying at your age. At your age, one should be a widower from at least one wife as a minimum. I'm a widower of four: Rosa, Manuela, Visitación and Enriqueta Gómez, who was the last one—nice-looking girls all of them—fond of flowers and fresh water. All, without exception, have felt this stick time and again. In my house—in my house it is sew and sing.

SHOEMAKER. Well, you can see for yourself what my life is. My wife . . . does not love me. She talks through the window with every one. Even with Don Blackbird, and it makes my blood boil.

MAYOR, *laughingly.* It's just that she's a merry little girl. It's only natural.

SHOEMAKER. Bah! I'm convinced . . . I believe she does this to torment me, because I'm sure . . . she hates me. First I thought I would tame her with my sweet character and my little presents: coral necklaces, little belts, tortoise-shell combs—even a pair of garters! But she—she's always herself!

MAYOR. And you, always yourself, devil take it! Come now, I see it, and it seems unbelievable how a man who calls himself a man can't dominate not one, but eighty females. If your wife talks through the window with every one, if she becomes bitter with you, it's because you want her to, because you have no comeback. Women should be squeezed at the waist, stepped upon strongly, and always shouted at. And if with all this they dare to say cock-a-doodle-doo, the stick; there's no other remedy. Rosa, Manuela, Visitación, and Enriqueta Gómez, who was the last one, can tell you that from the other world, if by any chance they happen to be there.

SHOEMAKER. But it so happens that there's one thing I don't dare to tell you.

Looks about cautiously.

MAYOR, *commandingly.* Say it!

SHOEMAKER. I understand it's a beastly thing, but—I'm not in love with my wife.

MAYOR. The devil!

SHOEMAKER. Yes, sir. The devil!

MAYOR. Then, you great rascal, why did you marry?

SHOEMAKER. There you have it. I can't explain it myself. My sister, my sister was to blame. "You're going to be left alone! You're going to this—you're going to I don't know what else!" I had a little money and my health, so I said: "Well, here goes!" But Lord help us. . . . Lightning strike my sister—may she rest in peace!

MAYOR. Well, you've certainly made a fool of yourself!

SHOEMAKER. Yes, sir—I have made a fool of myself. And now I can't stand it any longer. I didn't know what one woman was like. I say! And you . . . four! I'm too old to stand this hullabaloo.

WIFE, *singing within—lustily.*
> Let's have jaleo, jaleo!*
> Now that we're through with the riot,
> Let's have shooting, why be quiet;
> Let's have shooting, why be quiet!

SHOEMAKER. There you are!

MAYOR. And what do you intend to do?

SHOEMAKER. Fly the coop!

Makes a gesture.

MAYOR. Have you lost your senses?

SHOEMAKER, *excitedly.* This business of "shoemaker, stick to your last" is all over for me. I'm a peaceful man. I'm not

---
* Name of an old Spanish dance. "Jaleo" also means trouble, noise, hullabaloo.

used to all this shouting—and being talked about by everyone.

MAYOR, *laughing*. Consider what you have said you are
going to do; for you're able to do it—so don't be foolish.
It's a shame that a man like you should not have the
strength of character he ought.

*Through the door at the left the Shoemaker's Wife ap-
pears, powdering herself with a pink powder puff and
accentuating her eyebrows with a finger wet in her
mouth.*

WIFE. Good afternoon!

MAYOR. A very good afternoon.

To the Shoemaker.

How handsome! She's very handsome!

SHOEMAKER. You think so?

MAYOR. What well-placed roses you wear in your hair—
and how delightfully they smell!

WIFE. It's many that you have on the balconies of your
house.

MAYOR. Quite so. Do you like flowers?

WIFE. Me? Oh, I love them! I'd have flower pots on the
roof even—at the door—on the walls. But he—that one—
doesn't like them. Naturally, making boots all day, what
would you expect?

She sits at the window.

And good afternoon!

She looks toward the street and flirts.

SHOEMAKER. You see that?

MAYOR. A little bit brusque—but she's a very handsome
woman. What a pretty waist!

SHOEMAKER. You just don't know her.

MAYOR. Tssch!

Leaving majestically.

Until tomorrow! And let's see if that head of yours clears.
You, child, get some rest! What a pity! With such a figure!

Leaves, looking at the Shoemaker's Wife.

Because, my—those waves in her hair!

SHOEMAKER, *singing.*

> If your mother wants a king,
> In the deck there's a store.
> King of Diamonds, Clubs and Hearts,
> King of Spades—that makes four!

The Wife takes a chair and seated at the window begins to spin it.

SHOEMAKER, *taking another chair—and making it spin in the opposite direction.* You know that's a superstition of mine. You might just as well shoot me. Why do you do it?

WIFE, *letting go the chair.* What have I done? Didn't I tell you you don't even let me move.

SHOEMAKER. I'm tired of explaining to you—it's useless.

Starts to leave, but the Wife begins once more to spin her chair and the Shoemaker runs back from the door to spin his chair.

Woman, why don't you let me go?

WIFE. Heavens! Why it's just what I'm hoping—that you'd go.

SHOEMAKER. Then let me!

WIFE, *infuriated.* Well, go on!

Outside a flute is heard accompanied by a guitar playing an old polka with the rhythm comically accented. The Wife begins to nod her head in rhythm and the Shoemaker leaves through the left door.

WIFE, *singing.* La-ran, la-ran . . . Well, maybe I've just always liked the flute a lot. I've always been crazy about it. It almost makes me cry. What a delight! La-ran, la-ran. Listen. I wish he could hear it.

She rises and begins to dance as if she were doing it with imaginary suitors.

Oh, Emiliano! What beautiful little ribbons you have! No, no! It would embarrass poor little me. But, José María, don't you see that they're looking at us? Take a handkerchief then, for I don't want you to stain my dress. It's you I love, you. Ah, yes! Tomorrow when you bring the white mare, the one I like.

Laughs. The music stops.

Oh, too bad. That's just like leaving one with honey at her lips. How . . .

At the window Don Blackbird appears. He is dressed in a black swallow-tail coat and short breeches. His voice trembles and he moves his head like a wire doll.

DON BLACKBIRD. Ssst!

WIFE, *without looking, her back turned to the window, imitates a bird.* Caw, caw—cheep, cheep!

DON BLACKBIRD, *coming nearer.* Ssst! Little white Mistress Shoemaker, like the heart of an almond—but a little bit bitter, too. Little Mistress Shoemaker—burning golden reed —little Mistress Shoemaker, beautiful temptress of my heart.

WIFE. What a lot of things, Don Blackbird. I didn't know that big buzzards could talk. If there's a black blackbird fluttering around here—black and old—he'd better realize that I can't listen to him sing until later. Tweet, tweet— chirp, chirp.

DON BLACKBIRD. When the crepuscular shadows invade the world with their tenuous veils, and the public walk finds itself free of pedestrians, I shall return.

Takes snuff and sneezes on the Wife's back.

WIFE, *turning in irritation and hitting at Don Blackbird, who trembles.* A-h-h-h!!

Her face full of loathing.

And even if you don't return it'll be all right, indecent thing! Wire blackbird! Stove-lamp smudge! Run, now run! Did you ever see such a thing? Look what's sneezing! God go with you! How loathsome!

At the window the Youth with Sash stops. His straight-brim hat is down over his face and he shows signs of great sadness.

SASH YOUTH. Taking the air, Mistress Shoemaker?

WIFE. Exactly as you are.

SASH YOUTH. And always alone. What a pity!

WIFE, *sourly*. And why a pity?

SASH YOUTH. A woman like you—with that hair and that bosom so very beautiful . . .

WIFE, *more sourly*. But, why a pity?

SASH YOUTH. Because you're worthy of being painted on a picture postcard—and not to be just here—at this little window sill.

WIFE. Yes? I like postcards very much, especially those of sweethearts about to go on a trip.

SASH YOUTH. Oh, little Shoemaker's Wife, what a fever I have!

They continue talking.

SHOEMAKER, *entering, then retreating*. With the whole world, and at this hour! What will the people going to rosary at the church say? What will they say at the club? How they must talk about me! In each house they must discuss me—suit, underclothes and all.

Shoemaker's Wife laughs.

Oh, my lord! I have cause to leave! I'd like to listen to the wife of the sacristan. But the priests; what will the priests say? They are the ones I ought to hear.

He exits in desperation.

SASH YOUTH. How do you want me to say it? I love you, I love *thee* like . . .

WIFE. Really, that about "I love you, I love thee" has a style about it that makes me think someone is tickling me behind the ear with a feather. "I love thee, I love you."

SASH YOUTH. How many seeds has a sunflower?

WIFE. How should I know?

SASH YOUTH, *very near*. Every minute I sigh that many times for you, for *thee*.

WIFE, *brusquely*. Stop that. I can listen to you talk because I like it and it's pretty—but that's all, do you hear? A fine thing that would be!

SASH YOUTH. But that cannot be. Is it that you've given your word elsewhere?

WIFE. Now look here; go away.

SASH YOUTH. I won't move from this spot until you say yes. Oh, my little Shoemaker's Wife, give me your word!

Starts to embrace her.

WIFE, *closing the window violently.* What an impertinent man! What a fool! If I have turned your head you'll just have to bear it! As if I were here just to . . . just to . . . well, can't one talk to anybody in this town? From what I can see there are but two extremes in this town: either a nun or a dishrag. That's all I needed to know!

Pretending she smells something, running.

Oh, my dinner's on the stove! Evil woman!

It is growing dark. The Shoemaker enters wearing a great cape and with a bundle of clothes in his hand.

SHOEMAKER. I'm either another man or I don't know myself! Oh, my little house! Oh, my little bench! Wax, nails, calfskins . . . well.

He goes toward the door and retreats because he runs into the two Over-Pious Women.

FIRST OVER-PIOUS WOMAN. Resting, aren't you?

SECOND OVER-PIOUS WOMAN. You do well to rest!

SHOEMAKER, *in a bad humor.* Good night!

FIRST OVER-PIOUS WOMAN. To rest, master.

SECOND OVER-PIOUS WOMAN. To rest, to rest!

They leave.

SHOEMAKER. Yes, resting—but they weren't looking through the keyhole! Witches! Ugly things! Be careful of that insinuating tone in which you speak to me. Naturally, since in the whole village they talk of nothing else—he this, she that, the servants something else! Ay! May lightning strike my sister, may she rest in peace! But better alone than pointed at by everybody!

He goes out rapidly, leaving the door open. Through the left door the Wife appears.

WIFE. Supper's ready. Do you hear me?

Goes toward the door on the right.

Do you hear me? Well, has he had the courage to go to the café, leaving the door open? And without finishing the boots? Well, when he returns he'll listen to me! He'll have to listen! How like men, men are! How abusive and how . . . how . . . well!

Changing.

Oh, what a nice little breeze.

She lights the lamp and from the street comes the sound of the bells of the flock returning to the village. The Wife looks out the window.

What lovely flocks! I'm just crazy about little sheep. Look, look at that little white one that can just barely walk! Ay! But look at that big ugly one that keeps trampling on her and nothing . . .

Shouts.

Shepherd, day dreamer! Don't you see that they're stepping on the newborn lamb?

Pause.

Certainly it's my business. Why shouldn't it be my business? Big brute! You . . .

She moves away from the window.

Well, sir, where could that wandering man have gone? Well, if he delays two minutes more, I'll eat by myself, for I'm self-sufficient and more than that. With such a good supper as I've prepared! My stew with the fresh wild potatoes, two green peppers, white bread, a bit of lean bacon, and squash conserve with lemon peel on top. Because I have to take care of him! I have to take care of him! I take care of him by hand!

During all this monologue, she gives evidence of great activity, moving from one side to the other, arranging the chairs, taking lint off the curtains, and removing threads from her dress.

BOY, *at the door.* Are you still angry?

WIFE. My little darling of a neighbor, where are you going?

BOY, *at the door*. You won't scold me, will you? Because my mother, who sometimes beats me, I love twenty bushelfuls, but I love you thirty-two and a half.

WIFE. Why are you so lovely?

Seats him on her lap.

BOY. I came to tell you something that nobody else wants to tell you. "You go, you go, you go"—and no one wanted to go. And then, "Well, let the child go," they said—because it's some bad news that no one wants to carry.

WIFE. Then, tell me quickly. What has happened?

BOY. Well, don't be frightened—because it's not about dead people.

WIFE. Go on. . . .

BOY. Look, little Shoemaker's Wife!

Through the window a butterfly enters and the boy, getting down from her lap, begins to run after it.

A butterfly! A butterfly! Don't you have a hat? It's yellow with blue and red marks—and I don't know what all!

WIFE. But child, weren't you going to . . .?

BOY, *sternly*. Be quiet and speak in a low voice. Don't you see it will get frightened if you don't? Oh, give me your handkerchief!

WIFE, *already intrigued by the hunt*. Take it.

BOY. Shh! Don't stamp your feet.

WIFE. You're going to let it get away.

BOY, *in a low voice, as though charming the butterfly, sings*.

> Butterfly of the breezes,
> wind creature so lovely;
> butterfly of the breezes,
> wind creature so lovely;
> butterfly of the breezes,
> so green, so golden,
> a candle's flame;

butterfly of the breezes,
I beg you, stay there, stay there, stay there!
But you don't wish to linger,
to stay there an instant.
But you don't wish to linger,
to stay there an instant.
Butterfly of the breezes,
so green so golden,
a candle's flame;
butterfly of the breezes,
I beg you, stay there, stay there, stay there!
I beg you, stay there!
Butterfly, oh, please, are you there?

WIFE, *jokingly.* Ye-e-e-s.

BOY. No, now that's not fair.

The butterfly flies.

WIFE. Now! Now!

BOY, *running happily with the handkerchief.* Won't you light? Won't you quit flying?

WIFE, *also running on the other side.* It'll get away! It'll get away!

The Boy runs out the door pursuing the butterfly.

WIFE, *sternly.* Where are you going?

BOY, *suspended.* It's true.

Quickly.

But it's not my fault!

WIFE. Come now! Are you going to tell me what's happened? Quickly!

BOY. Oh! Well, look—your husband, the Shoemaker, has left never to return.

WIFE, *terrified.* What?

BOY. Yes, yes. He said that at my house before he got on the stagecoach. I saw him myself—and he told us to tell you that—and the whole town knows it.

WIFE, *sitting deflated.* But it isn't possible. It isn't possible! I don't believe it!

BOY. Yes, it's true; don't scold me!

WIFE, *rising in a fury, stamping on the floor*. And this is how he pays me? And this is how he pays me?

The Boy finds refuge behind the table.

BOY. Your hairpins are falling out!

WIFE. What's going to happen to me all alone in life? Oh! Oh! Oh!

The Boy runs out. The windows and the doors are full of Neighbors.

Yes, yes—come look at me! Rattlers, gossips! It's your fault. . . .

MAYOR. Look, now, be quiet. If your husband has left you—it was because you didn't love him—because it couldn't be.

WIFE. But, do you think you know more than I do? Yes, I did love him. I should say I loved him. How many good and rich suitors I had—and I never said yes to them. Oh, my poor thing—what things they must have told you!

SACRISTAN'S WIFE, *entering*. Woman, control yourself!

WIFE. I can't resign myself! I can't resign myself! Oh, Oh!

Neighbors dressed in various violent colors and carrying large glasses of cooling drinks begin to enter through the door. They turn, run, come and go, with the quickness and rhythm of a dance, around the Wife, who is sitting, shouting. The great skirts open with their turns. All adopt a comic attitude of pain.

NEIGHBOR IN YELLOW. A cooling drink?

RED NEIGHBOR. A little refreshment?

NEIGHBOR IN GREEN. For the blood?

NEIGHBOR IN BLACK. Lemon flavor?

NEIGHBOR IN PURPLE. Sarsaparilla?

RED NEIGHBOR. Mint is better.

PURPLE NEIGHBOR. Neighbor.

GREEN NEIGHBOR. Little neighbor.

BLACK NEIGHBOR. Shoemaker's Wife.

RED NEIGHBOR. Little Shoemaker's Wife.

The Neighbors create a great excitement. The Wife is crying at the top of her lungs.

CURTAIN

ACT TWO

The same set. To the left the abandoned cobbler's bench. To the right a counter with bottles and a pan behind which the Wife washes cups. She wears a burning-red dress with wide skirts. Her arms are bare. On the stage three tables. At one of them Don Blackbird is seated having a soft drink, and at the other the Youth with Hat, with his hat pulled down over his face.

The Wife washes glasses and cups with great ardor and places them on the counter. At the right appears the Sash Youth with hat as in Act One. He is sad. His arms hang at his sides and he looks at the Wife tenderly. If an actor exaggerates this character in the slightest he should be hit over the head by the director. No one should exaggerate. Farce always demands naturalness. The author has drawn the character and the tailor has dressed him. Simplicity. The Sash Youth stops at the door. Don Blackbird and the Hat Youth turn their heads to look at him. This is almost a movie scene. The glances and expressions taken together create the effect. The Wife stops washing and looks fixedly at the Sash Youth in the door. Silence.

WIFE. Come in.

SASH YOUTH. If you wish it.

WIFE, *amazed.* I? It absolutely does not matter to me one way or the other, but since I see you at the door . . .

SASH YOUTH. As you wish.

He leans on the counter. Between his teeth.

This is another one that I'm going to have to . . .

WIFE. What will you take?

SASH YOUTH. I'll follow your suggestions.

WIFE. Then—take the gate.

SASH YOUTH. Oh, Lord, how times change!

WIFE. Don't think I'm going to start crying. Come now. Are you going to have a drink? Coffee? A cold drink? What?

SASH YOUTH. A cold drink.

WIFE. Don't look at me so hard—you'll make me spill the syrup.

SASH YOUTH. It's only—I'm dying. Ay!

Past the window go two girls with immense fans. They look, cross themselves, scandalized, cover their eyes with their fans, and cross on with tiny steps.

WIFE. The drink.

SASH YOUTH, *looking at her.* Ay!

HAT YOUTH, *looking at the floor.* Ay!

DON BLACKBIRD, *looking at the ceiling.* Ay!

WIFE, *turns her head toward each of the three "ays."* "Ay" some more! But what is this—a tavern or a hospital? Abusers! If I didn't have to earn my living with these little wines and sweets—because I'm alone since the poor little husband of my soul left me, through the fault of all of you—how would it be possible for me to bear this? What do you say to that? I'm going to have to throw you out into the nice, wide street.

DON BLACKBIRD. Well said; very well said.

HAT YOUTH. You have opened a tavern and we can stay inside here as long as we want.

WIFE, *fiercely.* What? What?

The Sash Youth starts to leave and Don Blackbird rises smiling and acting as if he were in on the secret, and would return.

HAT YOUTH. Just what I said!

WIFE. Well whatever you say—I can say more. And you might as well know, and the whole village, that my husband has been gone four months, but that I'll never give in to anybody—never! Because a married woman should keep her place as God commands, and I'm not afraid of anybody; do you hear? For I have the blood of my grandfather, may he be in heaven, who was a horse tamer and what is called a man. Decent I was and decent I will be. I gave my word to my husband. Well, until death.

Don Blackbird goes rapidly to the door making motions that indicate a relation between him and the Wife.

HAT YOUTH, *rising.* I'm so angry I could take a bull by the horns, bend his head to the ground, eat his brains raw with my teeth, and surely not tire myself with biting.

He strides out rapidly and Don Blackbird flees toward the left.

WIFE, *with her hands to her head.* Lord, Lord, Lord and Lord!

She sits.

Through the door the Boy enters. He goes toward the Wife and covers her eyes.

BOY. Who am I?

WIFE. My child, little shepherd of Bethlehem.

BOY. I'm here.

They kiss.

WIFE. Did you come for your snack?

BOY. If you want to give me something.

WIFE. I have a piece of chocolate today.

BOY. Yes? I like to be in your house very much.

WIFE, *giving him the chocolate.* Aren't you just a little selfish?

BOY. Selfish? Do you see this black-and-blue spot on my knee?

WIFE. Let me see.

She sits on a low chair and takes the Boy in her arms.

BOY. Well, Cunillo did it because he was singing the couplets they made up about you and I hit him in the face, and then he threw a rock at me that—bang! Look.

WIFE. Does it hurt very much?

BOY. Not now, but I cried.

WIFE. Don't pay any attention to what they say.

BOY. Well, they were saying very indecent things. In-decent things that I know how to say, you understand. But that I don't want to say.

WIFE, *laughing.* Because if you say them I'll take a hot pimiento and make your tongue like a red-hot coal.

They laugh.

BOY. But—why should they blame you because your hus-band left?

WIFE. They, they are the ones to blame, and the ones who make me unhappy.

BOY, *sadly.* Don't say that, little cobbler's wife.

WIFE. I used to see myself in his eyes. When I'd see him coming mounted on his white mare . . .

BOY, *interrupting her.* Ha-ha-ha! You're fooling me. Mr. Shoemaker didn't have a mare.

WIFE. Boy, be more respectful. He had a mare; certainly he had one—but you . . . you weren't born yet.

BOY, *stroking his face.* Oh! That was it!

WIFE. You see, when I met him I was washing clothes in the little brook. Through half a yard of water the pebbles on the bottom could be seen laughing—laughing with little tremblings. He wore a tight black suit, a red tie of the finest silk, and four gold rings that shone like four suns.

BOY. How pretty!

WIFE. He looked at me and I looked at him. I lay back on the grass. I think I can still feel on my face that little fresh breeze that came through the trees. He stopped his horse and the horse's tail was white and so long that it reached down to the water in the brook.

The Wife is almost weeping. A distant song begins to be heard.

I was so flustered that I let two lovely handkerchiefs, just this tiny, flow down with the current.

BOY. How funny!

WIFE. He then said to me . . .

The song is heard nearer. Pause.

Shh!

BOY, *rises*. The couplets.

WIFE. The couplets.

Pause. The two listen.

Do you know what they say?

BOY, *gesturing with his hand*. Well, sort of.

WIFE. Well, sing them, then, because I want to know.

BOY. What for?

WIFE. So that I can find out once and for all what they're saying.

BOY, *singing and marking time*. You'll see:
>   Mistress Cobbler, Mistress Cobbler,
>   since her husband ran away,
>   since her husband ran away,
>   turned her house into a tavern
>   where the men go night and day,
>   where the men go night and day.

WIFE. They'll pay for this!

BOY, *beats time on the table with his hand*.
>   Who has bought you, Mistress Cobbler,
>   all those dresses may we guess,
>   all those dresses may we guess?
>   Cambrics, batistes, bobbin laces
>   fit for a proprietress,
>   fit for a proprietress.
>
>   Now she's courted by the Mayor,
>   now it is Don Blackbird's turn,
>   now it is Don Blackbird's turn.
>   Mistress Cobbler, Mistress Cobbler,
>   Mistress, you have men to burn,
>   Mistress, you have men to burn!

The voices can be heard near and clearly with their accompaniment of tambourines. The Wife takes up a Manila scarf and throws it over her shoulders.

Where are you going?

Frightened.

WIFE. They're going to drive me to buying a revolver!

The song grows faint. She runs to the door. But she bumps into the Mayor, who comes in majestically, beating on the floor with his staff.

MAYOR. Who waits on one here?

WIFE. The devil!

MAYOR. But what's happened?

WIFE. Something you must have known for several days. Something that you as Mayor ought not to allow. The people sing couplets to me, the neighbors laugh at their doors, and since I have no husband to watch out for me I'm going to defend myself—since in this town the authorities are pumpkin-heads, good-for-nothings, figureheads!

BOY. Very well said.

MAYOR, *severely.* Child, child! Enough of this shouting. Do you know what I've just done? Well, I put in jail two or three of those who came along singing.

WIFE. I'd like to see that!

VOICE, *outside.* So-n-n-y-y!

BOY. My mother's calling me!

Runs to the window.

Wha-a-a-t? Good-by. If you want, I can bring you my grandfather's big sword—the one who went to war. I can't lift it, you see, but you can.

WIFE, *smiling.* Whatever you want!

VOICE, *outside.* So-n-n-y-y!

BOY, *already in the street.* Wha-a-at?

MAYOR. From what I can see, that precocious and unnatural child is the only person in the village you treat well.

WIFE. You people can't say a single word that isn't an insult. And what is your most illustrious self laughing about?

MAYOR. To see you so beautiful but going to waste!

WIFE. Rather a dog!

Serves him a glass of wine.

MAYOR. What a disillusioning world! I've known many women just like poppies—like fragrant roses—dark women with eyes like inky fire, women whose hair smells of sweet oils and whose hands are always very warm, women whose waists you can encircle with these two fingers; but like you —there's no one like you. Day before yesterday I was sick all morning because I saw laid out on the grass two of your chemises with sky-blue ribbons—and it was like seeing you, Cobbler's Wife of my soul.

WIFE, *exploding furiously*. Be quiet, old man. Shut up! With grown daughters and a large family you shouldn't come courting in a manner so indecent and so bold-faced.

MAYOR. I'm a widower.

WIFE. And I'm a married woman!

MAYOR. But your husband has left you and will not return I'm sure.

WIFE. I'll live as if I still had him.

MAYOR. Well then, I can testify, because he told me, that he didn't love you even as much as this.

WIFE. Well, I can testify that your four wives—may lightning strike them—hated you to death.

MAYOR, *striking the floor with his staff*. Now that's enough!

WIFE, *throwing a glass*. Now that's enough!

Pause.

MAYOR, *under his breath*. If I could have you for my own, I'd show you how I could tame you!

WIFE, *coyly*. What's that you're saying?

MAYOR. Nothing. I was just thinking that if you were as good as you ought to be, you should understand I have the will and the generosity to make out a deed before a notary for a very beautiful house.

WIFE. And what of that?

MAYOR. With a drawingroom suite of furniture that cost five thousand reales, with centerpieces on the tables, brocade curtains, full-length mirrors . . .

WIFE. And what else?

MAYOR, *in the manner of a Don Juan.* The house has a bed with a canopy upheld by copper birds and daisies, a garden with six palms and a leaping fountain, but waits—in order to be happy—for a person I know to want to take possession of those rooms where she would be . . .

Addressing the Wife directly.

Look, you'd be like a Queen!

WIFE, *coyly.* I'm not used to such luxury. You sit down in the drawing room, crawl into the bed, look in the mirror, and lie with your mouth open underneath the palm trees waiting for the dates to fall—because I'm not giving up being a shoemaker's wife.

MAYOR, *in an affected tone of voice.* Nor am I giving up being Mayor. But it's time you knew that daylight won't break any earlier just for our disdaining it.

WIFE. And it's time you knew that I don't like you or any one in the village. An old man like you!

MAYOR, *indignant.* I'll end by putting you in jail.

WIFE. Just you dare!

Outside there is heard a trumpet call—florid and most comical.

MAYOR. What could that be?

WIFE, *happy and wide-eyed.* Puppets!

She beats her knees. Two women cross the window.

RED NEIGHBOR. Puppets!

PURPLE NEIGHBOR. Puppets!

BOY, *at the window.* Do you think they have any monkeys? Let's go!

WIFE, *to the Mayor.* I'm going to close up.

BOY. They're coming to your house.

WIFE. Yes?

Goes toward the door.

BOY. Look at them!

*At the door the Shoemaker, disguised, appears. He car-
ries a trumpet and a scroll at his back. The people
surround him. The Wife waits with great expectancy
and the Boy leaps in through the window and holds on
to her skirts.*

SHOEMAKER. Good afternoon!

WIFE. Good afternoon to you, Mr. Puppeteer.

SHOEMAKER. May a person rest here?

WIFE. And drink if you like.

MAYOR. Enter, my good man. And drink what you like,
for I'll pay.

To the Neighbors.

And you others, what are you doing here?

RED NEIGHBOR. Since we are out in the broad street, I
don't believe we're in your way.

*The Shoemaker, looking at all with calmness, leaves the
scroll on the table.*

SHOEMAKER. Let them be, Mr. Mayor—for I imagine you
are he—I must make my living with these people.

BOY. Where have I heard this man talk before?

*Throughout all this scene the Boy looks at the Shoemaker
with a puzzled air.*

Work your puppets!

The Neighbors laugh.

SHOEMAKER. As soon as I drink a glass of wine.

WIFE, *happily.* But are you going to work them in my
house?

SHOEMAKER. If you will permit me.

RED NEIGHBOR. Then, may we come in?

WIFE, *serious.* You can come in.

Gives a glass to the Shoemaker.

RED NEIGHBOR, *seating herself.* Now we shall enjoy ourselves a little.

The Mayor sits.

MAYOR. Do you come from very far?

SHOEMAKER. From very far.

MAYOR. From Seville?

SHOEMAKER. Leagues farther.

MAYOR. From France?

SHOEMAKER. Leagues farther.

MAYOR. From England?

SHOEMAKER. From the Philippine Islands.

The Neighbors give signs of admiration. The Wife is ecstatic.

MAYOR. You must have seen the Insurrectionists, then?

SHOEMAKER. Just the same as I am looking at you now.

BOY. And what are they like?

SHOEMAKER. Unbearable. Just imagine, almost all of them are shoemakers.

The Neighbors look at the Wife.

WIFE, *blushing.* And aren't they in any other profession?

SHOEMAKER. Absolutely not. In the Philippines—shoemakers!

WIFE. Well, perhaps in the Philippines shoemakers are stupid, but in this country there are some who are smart—and very smart at that.

RED NEIGHBOR, *flatteringly.* Very well spoken.

WIFE, *brusquely.* No one asked your opinion.

RED NEIGHBOR. But, child!

SHOEMAKER, *sternly, interrupting.* What rich wine!

Louder.

What rich wine indeed!

Silence.

Wine from grapes black as the souls of some women I have known.

WIFE. If any of them had souls!

MAYOR. Shh! And of what does your work consist?

SHOEMAKER, *empties the glass, smacks his tongue, looks at his wife.* Ah! It is a work of small show but much science. I present life from within. There are the couplets of the "Henpecked Shoemaker," and "Fierabras of Alexandria," "Life of Don Diego Corrientes," "Adventures of the Handsome Francisco Esteban," and above all, "The Art of Closing the Mouths of Gossipy and Impudent Women."

WIFE. My poor husband knew all those things!

SHOEMAKER. May God forgive him!

WIFE. Now you listen . . .

The Neighbors laugh.

BOY. Hush!

MAYOR, *imperiously.* Quiet! These are teachings that apply to everybody.

To the Shoemaker.

Whenever you wish.

The Shoemaker unrolls the scroll on which the story is painted, divided into tiny squares, drawn in red ochre and violent colors. The Neighbors start moving closer, and the Wife takes the Boy upon her knees.

SHOEMAKER. Attention.

BOY. Oh, how pretty!

Embraces the Wife. Murmurs are heard.

WIFE. Now pay good attention in case I don't understand everything.

BOY. It's surely not harder than sacred history.

SHOEMAKER. Worthy spectators. Listen to the true and moving ballad of the rubicund wife and the poor, patient little husband, that it may serve as warning and example to all the people of this world.

In a lugubrious tone.

Prick up your ears and understanding.

The Neighbors crane their necks, and a few of the women take hands.

BOY. Doesn't the puppeteer remind you of your husband when he talks?

WIFE. He had a sweeter voice.

SHOEMAKER. Are we ready?

WIFE. I feel a little shiver.

BOY. Me too!

SHOEMAKER, *pointing with a staff*.

> In Córdoba within a cottage
> set about with trees and rosebays,
> once upon a time a tanner
> lived there with the tanner's wife.

Expectancy.

> She a very stubborn woman—
> he a man of gentle patience;
> though the wife had not turned twenty,
> he was then well over fifty.
> Holy Lord, how they would argue!
> Look now at that beastly woman,
> laughing at the poor weak husband
> with her glances and her speaking.

On the scroll is drawn a woman who looks infantile and care-worn.

WIFE, *murmurs*. What an evil woman!

SHOEMAKER.

> Dark hair worthy of an empress
> had this little tanner's wife,
> and her flesh was like the water
> from Lucena's crystal sources.
> When she moved her skirts and flounces,
> as she walked about in springtime,
> all her clothes gave off the fragrance
> lemon groves and mint exhale.
> Oh what lemons, lemons
> of the lemon grove!
> Oh what a delicious
> little tannner's wife!

The Neighbors laugh.

> And now look how she was courted
> by young men of striking presence
> riding sleek and shining stallions
> harnessed in fine silken tassels.
> Elegant and charming persons
> would come riding past the doorway,
> flaunting with intent the luster
> of their coin-hung golden watch chains.
> And the tanner's wife was willing
> to converse with all these worthies,
> while the mares they rode went prancing
> on the cobbles of the roadway.
> Mark her how with one she's flirting,
> dressed and combed with fullest grooming,
> while the poor long-suffering tanner
> sticks his awl into the leather.

Very dramatically, joining his hands.

> Old and decent-acting husband,
> married to a wife too youthful,
> who could be that scoundrel horseman
> come to steal love from your doorway?

The Wife, who has been sighing, bursts into tears.

SHOEMAKER, *turning.* What's happened to you?

MAYOR. But, child!

Beats with his staff on the floor.

RED NEIGHBOR. A person who has something to shut up about always bawls.

PURPLE NEIGHBOR. Please go on!

The Neighbors murmur and shush.

WIFE. It's just that I'm filled with pity and can't contain myself. You see? I can't contain myself.

Weeps, trying to control herself, hiccuping most comically.

MAYOR. Quiet!

BOY. You see?

SHOEMAKER. Do me the favor of not interrupting. How well one can tell you're not trying to repeat something from memory!

BOY, *sighing*. How true!

SHOEMAKER, *ill-humored*.

> So, upon a Monday morning,
> just about eleven-thirty,
> when the sun left without shadow
> honeysuckle vines and rushes,
> when most happy danced together
> winds and thyme plants on the mountain,
> and the leaves of green were falling
> from the wild strawberry trees,
> there the spoiled wife was watering
> gilliflowers in her garden.
> Just then came her suitor riding,
> riding a Cordovan mare,
> and he told her through his sighing:
> "Sweetheart, if you only wished it,
> we'd have supper this next evening,
> we alone, but at your table."
> "Yes, but what about my husband?"
> "Husband? He won't know about it."
> "Then what will you do?" "I'll kill him."
> "He's a quick one, you might fail.
> Have you a revolver?" "Better!
> I can use a barber's razor."
> "Does it cut much?" "More than cold wind."

The Wife covers her eyes and squeezes the Boy. All the Neighbors are in a high pitch of expectancy which is shown by their expressions.

> And the blade's without a nick yet."
> "You're not lying?" "No, I'll give him
> ten quite well-directed blade thrusts
> in the following distribution,
> which I really think stupendous:
> four upon the lumbar region,
> one just at his left side nipple,

       one more at a place just like it,
       two on each side of his buttocks."
       "Will you kill him right away?"
       "This same night when he's returning
       with his leather and his horsehair,
       where the water ditch starts curving."

During this last verse, quickly, there is heard offstage a most loud and anguished shout; the Neighbors rise. Another shout nearer. The scroll and the staff fall from the hands of the Shoemaker. All tremble comically.

BLACK NEIGHBOR, *at the window.* They've drawn their knives!

WIFE. Oh, my Lord!

RED NEIGHBOR. Holiest Virgin!

SHOEMAKER. What a row!

BLACK NEIGHBOR. They're killing themselves! They're ripping each other to pieces—all through the fault of that woman!

Points to the Wife.

MAYOR, *nervous.* Let's go see.

BOY. I'm very scared!

GREEN NEIGHBOR. Come on! Come on!

They start leaving.

VOICE, *outside.* Because of that evil woman!

SHOEMAKER. I can't stand this! I can't stand it!

Runs around the stage with his hands at his head.

All are leaving rapidly, exclaiming and casting looks of hate toward the Wife. She quickly closes the window and door.

WIFE. Have you ever seen such hatefulness? I swear by the holiest blood of our Father Jesus that I'm innocent. Ay! What could have happened? Look, look how I'm trembling.

Shows him her hands.

It seems as if my hands want to fly off by themselves.

SHOEMAKER. Be calm, girl. Is your husband in the street?

WIFE, *bursting into sobs*. My husband? Oh, Mr. Puppeteer!

SHOEMAKER. What's the matter?

WIFE. My husband left me because of these people and now I'm alone—with nobody's warmth.

SHOEMAKER. Poor little thing.

WIFE. And I loved him so much! I adored him!

SHOEMAKER, *starting*. That isn't true!

WIFE, *quickly ceasing her sobs*. What did you say?

SHOEMAKER. I said it's such an incomprehensible thing that . . . it doesn't seem to be true.

Disturbed.

WIFE. You're very right, but since then I haven't been able to eat or sleep, or live; because he was my happiness, my defense.

SHOEMAKER. And, loving him as much as you did, did he abandon you? I can see from that your husband was not very understanding.

WIFE. Please keep your tongue in your pocket. No one has given you permission to voice your opinion.

SHOEMAKER. You must excuse me; I didn't mean to . . .

WIFE. The idea! Why, he was so smart!

SHOEMAKER, *jokingly*. Ye-e-e-s?

WIFE, *sternly*. Yes. You know those ballads and little songs you sing and tell through the villages? Well, that isn't anything to what he knew. He knew—three times as much!

SHOEMAKER, *serious*. That can't be.

WIFE, *sternly*. Four times as much! He used to tell them all to me when we went to bed. Old stories that you probably haven't even heard mentioned,

Coyly.

and I would get so frightened. But he would say to me: "Darling of my soul, these are just tiny little white lies!"

SHOEMAKER, *indignant*. That's not true.

WIFE, *surprised*. Eh? Have you lost your mind?

SHOEMAKER. It's a lie!

WIFE, *angry*. What are you saying, you puppeteer of the devil?

SHOEMAKER, *strongly, standing*. That your husband was quite right. Those stories are just lies—fantasy, that's all.

WIFE, *sourly*. Naturally, my good sir. You seem to take me for a complete fool—but you won't deny that these stories make an impression.

SHOEMAKER. Ah, that is flour of another sack, then! They make an impression on impressionable souls.

WIFE. Every one has feelings.

SHOEMAKER. According to how one looks at it. I've known many people without feelings. And in my town there lived a woman at one time who had a heart so unfeeling that she would talk to her friends through the window while her husband made boots and shoes from morning to night.

WIFE, *rising and taking up a chair*. Are you saying that because of me?

SHOEMAKER. What?

WIFE. If you were going to add anything else, go ahead! Be brave!

SHOEMAKER, *humbly*. Miss, what are you saying? How do I know who you are? I haven't insulted you in any way. Why do you treat me so? But that's my fate!

Almost weeping.

WIFE, *stern, but moved*. Look here, my good man; I spoke like that because I'm on pins and needles. Everybody besieges me—everybody criticizes me. How can I help but be looking for the slightest opportunity to defend myself? Because I'm alone, because I'm young, and yet already live only for my memories. . . .

Weeps.

SHOEMAKER, *weepily*. I understand, you lovely young creature. I understand much better than you can imagine, because—you must know, most confidentially, that your situation is—yes, there's no doubt of it—identical with mine.

WIFE, *intrigued*. Could that be possible?

SHOEMAKER, *lets himself fall across the table*, I—was abandoned by my wife!

WIFE. Death would be too good for her!

SHOEMAKER. She dreamt of a world that was not mine. She was flighty and domineering; she loved conversation, and the sweets I could not buy for her, too much, and on a day that was stormy with a wind like a hurricane, she left me forever.

WIFE. And why do you wander over the world now?

SHOEMAKER. I search for her to forgive her and to live out with her the short time I have left in this world. At my age one is rather insecurely in this world of God's.

WIFE, *quickly*. Take a little hot coffee; it'll be good for you after all this hullabaloo.

Goes to the counter to pour the coffee and turns her back on the Shoemaker.

SHOEMAKER, *crossing himself exaggeratedly and opening his eyes*. May God repay you, my little red carnation.

WIFE, *offers him the cup. She keeps the saucer in her hand. He drinks in gulps*. Is it good?

SHOEMAKER, *flatteringly*. Since it was made by your hands!

WIFE, *smiling*. Thank you!

SHOEMAKER, *with a final swallow*. Oh, how I envy your husband!

WIFE. Why?

SHOEMAKER, *gallantly*. Because he married the most beautiful woman in the world!

WIFE, *softened*. What things you say!

SHOEMAKER. And now I'm almost glad I have to go, because here you are alone, and I'm alone, and you so beautiful and I, having a tongue—it seems to me that I couldn't help making a certain suggestion. . . .

WIFE, *recovering.* My heavens, stop that! What do you think? I keep my whole heart for that wanderer, for the one whom I must, for my husband!

SHOEMAKER, *very pleased—throwing his hat on the ground.* That's fine! Spoken like a real woman—fine!

WIFE, *joking a little, surprised.* It seems to me that you're a little . . .

Points to her temple.

SHOEMAKER. Whatever you say. But understand that I'm not in love with anyone except my wife, my lawfully wedded wife!

WIFE. And I with my husband; and nobody but my husband. How many times I've said it for even the deaf to hear. . . .

With her hands folded.

Oh, Shoemaker of my soul!

SHOEMAKER, *aside.* Oh, wife of my soul!

There is knocking at the door.

WIFE. Heavens! One is in a constant state of excitement. Who is it?

BOY. Open!

WIFE. How's this? How did you get here?

BOY. Oh, I've come running to tell you!

WIFE. What's happened?

BOY. Two or three young men have wounded each other with knives and they're blaming you for it. Wounds that bleed a lot. All the women have gone to see the judge to make you leave town. Oh! And the men wanted the sacristan to ring the bells so they could sing you the couplets. . . .

The Boy is panting and perspiring.

WIFE, *to the Shoemaker.* Do you see that?

BOY. All the plaza is full of people talking—it's like the fair—and all of them are against you!

SHOEMAKER. Villains! I'm of a mind to go out and defend you.

WIFE. What for? They'd just put you in jail. I'm the one who's going to have to do something drastic.

BOY. From the window in your room you can see the excitement in the plaza.

WIFE, *in a hurry*. Come on, I want to see for myself the hatefulness of those people.

Runs out quickly.

SHOEMAKER. Yes, yes, villains! But I'll soon settle accounts with all of them and they'll have to answer to me. Oh, my little house! What a pleasant warmth comes from your doors and windows! Oh what terrible holes, what bad meals, what dirty sheets out along the world's highways. And how stupid not to realize that my wife was pure gold, the best in the world! It makes me almost want to weep!

RED NEIGHBOR, *entering rapidly*. Good man.

YELLOW NEIGHBOR, *rapidly*. Good man.

RED NEIGHBOR. Leave this house immediately. You are a decent person and ought not to be here.

YELLOW NEIGHBOR. This is the house of a lioness, of a she-hyena.

RED NEIGHBOR. Of an evil-born woman, betrayer of men.

YELLOW NEIGHBOR. But she'll either leave town or we'll put her out. She's driving us crazy.

RED NEIGHBOR. I'd like to see her dead.

YELLOW NEIGHBOR. In her shroud, with flowers on her breast.

SHOEMAKER, *anguished*. That's enough!

RED NEIGHBOR. Blood has been shed.

YELLOW NEIGHBOR. There are no white handkerchiefs left.

RED NEIGHBOR. Two men like two suns.

YELLOW NEIGHBOR. Pierced by knives.

SHOEMAKER, *loudly*. Enough now!

RED NEIGHBOR. All because of her.

YELLOW NEIGHBOR. Her, her, her!

RED NEIGHBOR. We are really looking out for your good.

YELLOW NEIGHBOR. We're letting you know in time.

SHOEMAKER. You big liars! Evil-born women! Hypocrites! I'm going to drag you by the hair. . . .

RED NEIGHBOR, *to the other.* She's captured him too.

YELLOW NEIGHBOR. Her kisses must have done it.

SHOEMAKER. May the devil take you! Basilisks, perjurers!

BLACK NEIGHBOR, *at the window.* Neighbor, run!

Leaves running. The two Neighbors do likewise.

RED NEIGHBOR. Another one ensnared.

YELLOW NEIGHBOR. Another one!

SHOEMAKER. Harpies! Jewesses! I'll put barber's razors in your shoes. You'll have bad dreams about me.

BOY, *entering rapidly.* A group of men was just going into the Mayor's house. I'm going to hear what they're saying.

Exits running.

WIFE, *entering, courageously.* Well, here I am, if they dare to come. And with the composure of one descended from a family of horsemen who many times crossed the wilds without saddles—bareback on their horses.

SHOEMAKER. And will not your fortitude sometime weaken?

WIFE. Never. A person like me, who is sustained by love and honor, never surrenders. I am able to hold out here until all my hair turns white.

SHOEMAKER, *moved, advancing toward her.* Oh . . .

WIFE. What's the matter with you?

SHOEMAKER. I am overcome. . . .

WIFE. Look, the whole town is after me; they want to come kill me, yet I'm not the least afraid. A knife is answered with a knife, and a club with a club, but at night, when I close this door and go to my bed—I feel such sadness—what sadness! And I suffer such smotherings! The bureau creaks—I start! The windows sound with the rain against them—another start! Without meaning to, I shake the bed hangings myself—double start! And all this is nothing more than fear of loneliness and its phantoms, which I have not seen because I have not wanted to, but which my mother and grandmother and all the women of my family who have had eyes have seen.

SHOEMAKER. And why don't you change your way of living?

WIFE. Are you crazy? What can I do? Where can I go? Here I am and God will say what is to happen.

Outside, distantly, murmurs and applause are heard.

SHOEMAKER. Well, I'm sorry, but I must be on my way before night falls. How much do I owe you?

Takes up the scroll.

WIFE. Nothing.

SHOEMAKER. I couldn't.

WIFE. It's on the house.

SHOEMAKER. Many thanks.

Puts the scroll to his back sadly.

Then, good-by—forever; because at my age . . .

He is moved.

WIFE, *reacting.* I wouldn't want to say good-by like this. I am usually very gay.

In a clear voice.

Good man, may God will that you find your wife so that you may once more live with the care and decency that you were used to.

She is moved.

SHOEMAKER. I say the same about your husband. But, you know, the world is small: what do you want me to say to him if I meet him by chance in my wanderings?

WIFE. Tell him I adore him.

SHOEMAKER, *coming near.* And what else?

WIFE. That in spite of his fifty and some odd years, his most blessed fifty years, I find him more slender and graceful than all the men in the world.

SHOEMAKER. Child, how wonderful you are! You love him as much as I love my wife!

WIFE. Much more!

SHOEMAKER. That's not possible. I'm like a little puppy, and my wife commands in the castle. But let her command! She has more sense than I have.

He is near and as though praying to her.

WIFE. And don't forget to tell him I'm waiting for him, for the nights are long in winter.

SHOEMAKER. Then, you would receive him well?

WIFE. As if he were the king and queen together.

SHOEMAKER, *trembling*. And if he should by chance come right now?

WIFE. I would go mad with happiness!

SHOEMAKER. Would you forgive him his craziness?

WIFE. How long ago I forgave him!

SHOEMAKER. Do you want him to come back now?

WIFE. Oh, if he would only come!

SHOEMAKER, *shouting*. Well, he's here.

WIFE. What are you saying?

SHOEMAKER, *removing his glasses and the disguise*. I can't bear it any longer! Wife of my heart!

The Wife is as though insane, with her arms held away from her body. The Shoemaker embraces her, and she looks at him intently in this critical moment. Outside, the murmuring of the couplets is clearly heard.

VOICE, *without*.

> Mistress Cobbler, Mistress Cobbler,
> since her husband ran away,
> since her husband ran away,
> turned her house into a tavern
> where the men go night and day,
> where the men go night and day.

WIFE, *recovering.* Loafer, scoundrel, rascal, villain! Do you hear that? All because of you!

Begins throwing chairs.

SHOEMAKER, *full of emotion, going toward the bench.* Wife of my heart!

WIFE. Vagabond! Oh, how happy I am you've returned! What a life I'm going to lead you! Not even the Inquisition could have been worse. Not even the Templars at Rome!

SHOEMAKER, *at the bench.* House of my happiness!

The couplets are heard quite near. The Neighbors appear at the window.

VOICES, *outside.*

>   Who has bought you, Mistress Cobbler,
>   all those dresses may we guess,
>   all those dresses may we guess?
>   Cambrics, batistes, bobbin laces
>   fit for a proprietress,
>   fit for a proprietress.
>
>   Now she's courted by the Mayor,
>   now it is Don Blackbird's turn,
>   now it is Don Blackbird's turn.
>   Mistress Cobbler, Mistress Cobbler,
>   Mistress, you have men to burn,
>   Mistress, you have men to burn!

WIFE. How unfortunate I am! With this man God has given me!

Going to the door.

Quiet, long tongues, red Jews! And now, come ahead, come ahead if you want to. There are two of us now to defend my house. Two! Two! My husband and I.

To her husband.

Oh, this scoundrel, oh, this villain!

The noise of the couplets fills the stage. A bell begins to ring distantly and furiously.

CURTAIN

THE LOVE OF DON PERLIMPLÍN
AND BELISA IN THE GARDEN

AN EROTIC LACE-PAPER VALENTINE
IN FOUR SCENES
CHAMBER VERSION

(1931)

CHARACTERS

DON PERLIMPLÍN
BELISA
MARCOLFA
MOTHER OF BELISA
FIRST SPRITE
SECOND SPRITE

PROLOGUE

*House of Don Perlimplín. Green walls; chairs and fur-
niture painted black. At the rear, a deep window with balcony through which Belisa's balcony may be seen. A sonata
is heard. Perlimplín wears a green cassock and a white wig
full of curls. Marcolfa, the servant, wears the classic striped
dress.*

PERLIMPLÍN. Yes?

MARCOLFA. Yes.

PERLIMPLÍN. But why "yes"?

MARCOLFA. Just because yes.

PERLIMPLÍN. And if I should say no?

MARCOLFA, *acidly.* No?

PERLIMPLÍN. No.

MARCOLFA. Tell me, Master, the reason for that "no."

PERLIMPLÍN. You tell me, you persevering domestic, the
reasons for that "yes."

Pause.

MARCOLFA. Twenty and twenty are forty . . .

PERLIMPLÍN, *listening.* Proceed.

MARCOLFA. And ten, fifty.

PERLIMPLÍN. Go ahead.

MARCOLFA. At fifty years one is no longer a child.

PERLIMPLÍN. Of course!

MARCOLFA. I may die any minute.

PERLIMPLÍN. Good Lord!

MARCOLFA, *weeping.* And what will happen to you all
alone in the world?

PERLIMPLÍN. What will happen?

MARCOLFA. That's why you have to marry.

PERLIMPLÍN, *distracted*. Yes?

MARCOLFA, *sternly*. Yes.

PERLIMPLÍN, *miserably*. But Marcolfa . . . why "yes"? When I was a child a woman strangled her husband. He was a shoemaker. I can't forget it. I've always said I wouldn't marry. My books are enough for me. What good will marriage do me?

MARCOLFA. Marriage holds great charms, Master. It isn't what it appears on the outside. It's full of hidden things . . . things which it would not be becoming for a servant to mention. You see that . . .

PERLIMPLÍN. That what?

MARCOLFA. That I have blushed.

Pause. A piano is heard.

VOICE OF BELISA, *within, singing*.
>Ah love, ah love.
>Tight in my thighs imprisoned
>There swims like a fish the sun.
>Warm water in the rushes.
>Ah love.
>Morning cock, the night is going!
>Don't let it vanish, no!

MARCOLFA. My master will see the reason I have.

PERLIMPLÍN, *scratching his head*. She sings prettily.

MARCOLFA. She is the woman for my master. The fair Belisa.

PERLIMPLÍN. Belisa . . . but wouldn't it be better . . . ?

MARCOLFA. No. Now come.

She takes him by the hand and goes toward the balcony. Say, "Belisa."

PERLIMPLÍN. Belisa . . .

MARCOLFA. Louder.

PERLIMPLÍN. Belisa!

The balcony of the house opposite opens and Belisa appears, resplendent in her loveliness. She is half naked.

BELISA. Who calls?

Marcolfa hides behind the window curtains.

MARCOLFA. Answer!

PERLIMPLÍN, *trembling*. I was calling.

BELISA. Yes?

PERLIMPLÍN. Yes.

BELISA. But why, "yes"?

PERLIMPLÍN. Just because yes.

BELISA. And if I should say no?

PERLIMPLÍN. I would be sorry, because . . . we have decided that I want to marry.

BELISA, *laughs*. Marry whom?

PERLIMPLÍN. You.

BELISA, *serious*. But . . .

Calling.

Mamá! Mamá-á-á!

MARCOLFA. This is going well.

Enter the Mother wearing a great eighteenth-century wig full of birds, ribbons and glass beads.

BELISA. Don Perlimplín wants to marry me. What must I do?

MOTHER. The very best of afternoons to you, my charming little neighbor. I always said to my poor little girl that you have the grace and elegance of that great lady who was your mother, whom I did not have the pleasure of knowing.

PERLIMPLÍN. Thank you.

MARCOLFA, *furiously, from behind the curtain*. I have decided that we are going . . .

PERLIMPLÍN. We have decided that we are going . . .

MOTHER. To contract matrimony. Is that not so?

PERLIMPLÍN. That is so.

BELISA. But, Mamá, what about me?

MOTHER. You are agreeable, naturally. Don Perlimplín is a fascinating husband.

PERLIMPLÍN. I hope to be one, madam.

MARCOLFA, *calling to Don Perlimplín*. This is almost settled.

PERLIMPLÍN. Do you think so?

They whisper together.

MOTHER, *to Belisa*. Don Perlimplín has many lands. On these are many geese and sheep. The sheep are taken to market. At the market they give money for them. Money produces beauty . . . and beauty is sought after by all men.

PERLIMPLÍN. Then . . .

MOTHER. Ever so thrilled . . . Belisa . . . go inside. It isn't well for a maiden to hear certain conversations.

BELISA. Until later.

She leaves.

MOTHER. She is a lily. You've seen her face?

Lowering her voice.

But if you should see further! Just like sugar. But, pardon. I need not call these things to the attention of a person as modern and competent as you. . . .

PERLIMPLÍN. Yes?

MOTHER. Why, yes. I said it without irony.

PERLIMPLÍN. I don't know how to express our gratitude.

MOTHER. Oh, "our gratitude." What extraordinary delicacy! The gratitude of your heart and yourself . . . I have sensed it. I have sensed it . . . in spite of the fact that it is twenty years since I have had relations with a man.

MARCOLFA, *aside*. The wedding.

PERLIMPLÍN. The wedding . . .

MOTHER. Whenever you wish. Though . . .

She brings out a handkerchief and weeps.

. . . to every mother . . . until later!

Leaves.

MARCOLFA. At last!

PERLIMPLÍN. Oh, Marcolfa, Marcolfa! Into what world are you going to thrust me?

MARCOLFA. Into the world of matrimony.

PERLIMPLÍN. And if I should be frank, I would say that I feel thirsty. Why don't you bring me some water?

Marcolfa approaches him and whispers in his ear.

Who could believe it?

The piano is heard. The stage is in darkness. Belisa opens the curtains of her balcony, almost naked, singing languidly.

BELISA.

Ah love, ah love.
Tight in my warm thighs imprisoned,
There swims like a fish the sun.

MARCOLFA. Beautiful maiden.

PERLIMPLÍN. Like sugar . . . white inside. Will she be capable of strangling me?

MARCOLFA. Woman is weak if frightened in time.

BELISA.

Ah love, ah love.
Morning cock, the night is going!
Don't let it vanish, no!

PERLIMPLÍN. What does she mean, Marcolfa? What does she mean?

Marcolfa laughs.

What is happening to me? What is it?

The piano goes on playing. Past the balcony flies a band of black paper birds.

CURTAIN

SCENE 1

Don Perimplín's room. At the center there is a great bed topped by a canopy with plume ornaments. In the back wall there are six doors. The first one on the right serves as entrance and exit for Don Perlimplín. It is the wedding night.

Marcolfa, with a candelabrum in her hand, speaks at the first door on the left side.

MARCOLFA. Good night.

BELISA, *offstage.* Good night, Marcolfa.

Don Perlimplín enters, magnificently dressed.

MARCOLFA. May my master have a good wedding night.

PERLIMPLÍN. Good night, Marcolfa.

Marcolfa leaves. Perlimplín tiptoes toward the room in front and looks from the door.

Belisa, in all that froth of lace you look like a wave, and you give me the same fear of the sea that I had as a child. Since you came from the church my house is full of secret whispers, and the water grows warm by itself in the glasses. Oh! Perlimplín . . . Where are you, Perlimplín?

Leaves on tiptoe. Belisa appears, dressed in a great sleeping garment adorned with lace. She wears an enormous headdress which launches cascades of needlework and lace down to her feet. Her hair is loose and her arms bare.

BELISA. The maid perfumed this room with thyme and not with mint as I ordered. . . .

Goes toward the bed.

Nor did she put on the fine linen which Marcolfa has.

At this moment there is a soft music of guitars. Belisa crosses her hands over her breast.

Ah! Whoever seeks me ardently will find me. My thirst is never quenched, just as the thirst of the gargoyles who spurt water in the fountains is never quenched.

The music continues.

Oh, what music! Heavens, what music! Like the soft warm downy feathers of a swan! Oh! Is it I? Or is it the music?

She throws a great cape of red velvet over her shoulders and walks about the room. The music is silent and five whistles are heard.

BELISA. Five of them!

Perlimplín appears.

PERLIMPLÍN. Do I disturb you?

BELISA. How could that be possible?

PERLIMPLÍN. Are you sleepy?

BELISA, *ironically*. Sleepy?

PERLIMPLÍN. The night has become a little chilly.

Rubs his hands. Pause.

BELISA, *with decision*. Perlimplín.

PERLIMPLÍN, *trembling*. What do you want?

BELISA, *vaguely*. It's a pretty name, "Perlimplín."

PERLIMPLÍN. Yours is prettier, Belisa.

BELISA, *laughing*. Oh! Thank you!

Short pause.

PERLIMPLÍN. I wanted to tell you something.

BELISA. And that is?

PERLIMPLÍN. I have been late in deciding . . . but . . .

BELISA. Say it.

PERLIMPLÍN. Belisa, I love you.

BELISA. Oh, you little gentleman! That's your duty.

PERLIMPLÍN. Yes?

BELISA. Yes.

PERLIMPLÍN. But why "yes"?

BELISA, *coyly*. Because.

PERLIMPLÍN. No.

BELISA. Perlimplín!

PERLIMPLÍN. No, Belisa, before I married you, I didn't love you.

BELISA, *jokingly*. What are you saying?

PERLIMPLÍN. I married . . . for whatever reason, but I didn't love you. I couldn't have imagined your body until I saw it through the keyhole when you were putting on your wedding dress. And then it was that I felt love come to me. Then! Like the deep thrust of a lancet in my throat.

BELISA, *intrigued*. But, the other women?

PERLIMPLÍN. What women?

BELISA. Those you knew before.

PERLIMPLÍN. But are there other women?

BELISA, *getting up*. You astonish me!

PERLIMPLÍN. The first to be astonished was I.

Pause. The five whistles are heard.

What's that?

BELISA. The clock.

PERLIMPLÍN. Is it five?

BELISA. Bedtime.

PERLIMPLÍN. Do I have your permission to remove my coat?

BELISA. Of course,

Yawning.

little husband. And put out the light, if that is your wish.

Perlimplín puts out the light.

PERLIMPLÍN, *in a low voice*. Belisa.

BELISA, *loudly*. What, child?

PERLIMPLÍN, *whispering*. I've put the light out.

BELISA, *jokingly*. I see that.

PERLIMPLÍN, *in a much lower voice*. Belisa . . .

BELISA, *in a loud voice*. What, enchanter?

PERLIMPLÍN. I adore you!

The five whistles are heard much louder and the bed is uncovered. Two Sprites, entering from opposite sides of the stage, run a curtain of misty gray. The theater is left in darkness. Flutes sound with a sweet, sleepy tone. The Sprites should be two children. They sit on the prompt box facing the audience.

FIRST SPRITE. And how goes it with you in this tiny darkness?

SECOND SPRITE. Neither well nor badly, little friend.

FIRST SPRITE. Here we are.

SECOND SPRITE. And how do you like it? It's always nice to cover other people's failings . . .

FIRST SPRITE. And then to let the audience take care of uncovering them.

SECOND SPRITE. Because if things are not covered up with all possible precautions . . .

FIRST SPRITE. They would never be discovered.

SECOND SPRITE. And without this covering and uncovering . . .

FIRST SPRITE. What would the poor people do?

SECOND SPRITE, *looking at the curtain.* There must not even be a slit.

FIRST SPRITE. For the slits of today are darkness tomorrow.

They laugh.

SECOND SPRITE. When things are quite evident . . .

FIRST SPRITE. Man figures that he has no need to discover them . . . in them secrets he already knew.

SECOND SPRITE. And he goes to dark things to discover them . . . in them secrets he already knew.

FIRST SPRITE. But that's what we're here for. We Sprites!

SECOND SPRITE. Did you know Perlimplín?

FIRST SPRITE. Since he was a child.

SECOND SPRITE. And Belisa?

FIRST SPRITE. Very well. Her room exhaled such intense perfume that I once fell asleep and awoke between her cat's claws.

They laugh.

SECOND SPRITE. This affair was . . .

FIRST SPRITE. Oh, of course!

SECOND SPRITE. All the world thought so.

FIRST SPRITE. And the gossip must have turned then to more mysterious things.

SECOND SPRITE. That's why our efficient and most sociable screen should not be opened yet.

FIRST SPRITE. No, don't let them find out.

SECOND SPRITE. The soul of Perlimplín, tiny and frightened like a newborn duckling, becomes enriched and sublime at these moments.

They laugh.

FIRST SPRITE. The audience is impatient.

SECOND SPRITE. And with reason. Shall we go?

FIRST SPRITE. Let's go. I feel a fresh breeze on my back already.

SECOND SPRITE. Five cool camellias of the dawn have opened in the walls of the bedroom.

FIRST SPRITE. Five balconies upon the city.

They rise and throw on some great blue hoods.

SECOND SPRITE. Don Perlimplín, do we help or hinder you?

FIRST SPRITE. Help: because it is not fair to place before the eyes of the audience the misfortune of a good man.

SECOND SPRITE. That's true, little friend, for it's not the same to say: "I have seen," as "It is said."

FIRST SPRITE. Tomorrow the whole world will know about it.

SECOND SPRITE. And that's what we wish.

FIRST SPRITE. One word of gossip and the whole world knows.

SECOND SPRITE. Sh . . .

Flutes begin to sound.

FIRST SPRITE. Shall we go through this tiny darkness?

SECOND SPRITE. Let us go now, little friend.

FIRST SPRITE. Now?

SECOND SPRITE. Now.

They open the curtain. Don Perlimplín appears on the bed, with two enormous gilded horns. Belisa is at his side. The five balconies at the back of the stage are wide open, and through them the white light of dawn enters.

PERLIMPLÍN, *awakening.* Belisa! Belisa! Answer me!

BELISA, *pretending to awaken.* Perlimplinpinito . . . what do you want?

PERLIMPLÍN. Tell me quickly.

BELISA. What do you want me to tell you? I fell asleep long before you did.

PERLIMPLÍN, *leaps from the bed. He has on his cassock.* Why are the balconies open?

BELISA. Because this night the wind has blown as never before.

PERLIMPLÍN. Why do the balconies have five ladders that reach to the ground?

BELISA. Because that is the custom in my mother's country.

PERLIMPLÍN. And whose are those five hats which I see under the balconies?

BELISA, *leaping from the bed.* The little drunkards who come and go. Perlimplinillo! Love!

Perlimplín looks at her, staring stupefied.

PERLIMPLÍN. Belisa! Belisa! And why not? You explain everything so well. I am satisfied. Why couldn't it have been like that?

BELISA, *coyly.* I'm not a little fibber.

PERLIMPLÍN. And I love you more every minute!

BELISA. That's the way I like it.

PERLIMPLÍN. For the first time in my life I am happy!

He approaches and embraces her, but, in that instant, turns brusquely from her.

Belisa, who has kissed you? Don't lie, for I know!

BELISA, *gathering her hair and throwing it over her shoulder.* Of course you know! What a playful little husband I have!

In a low voice.

You! You have kissed me!

PERLIMPLÍN. Yes. I have kissed you . . . but . . . if someone else had kissed you . . . if someone else had kissed you . . . do you love me?

BELISA, *lifting a naked arm.* Yes, little Perlimplín.

PERLIMPLÍN. Then, what do I care?

He turns and embraces her.

Are you Belisa?

BELISA, *coyly, and in a low voice.* Yes! Yes! Yes!

PERLIMPLÍN. It almost seems like a dream!

BELISA, *recovering.* Look, Perlimplín, close the balconies because before long people will be getting up.

PERLIMPLÍN. What for? Since we have both slept enough, we shall see the dawn. Don't you like that?

BELISA. Yes, but . . .

She sits on the bed.

PERLIMPLÍN. I have never seen the sunrise.

Belisa, exhausted, falls on the pillows of the bed.

It is a spectacle which . . . this may seem an untruth . . . thrills me! Don't you like it?

Goes toward the bed.

Belisa, are you asleep?

BELISA, *in her dreams.* Yes.

Perlimplín tiptoes over and covers her with the red cape. An intense golden light enters through the balconies. Bands of paper birds cross them amidst the ringing of the morning bells. Perlimplín has seated himself on the edge of the bed.

PERLIMPLÍN.

> Love, love
> that here lies wounded.
> So wounded by love's going;
> so wounded,
> dying of love.
> Tell every one that it was just
> the nightingale.
> A surgeon's knife with four sharp edges;
> the bleeding throat—forgetfulness.
> Take me by the hands, my love,
> for I come quite badly wounded,
> so wounded by love's going.
> So wounded!
> Dying of love!

CURTAIN

SCENE 2

Perlimplín's dining room. The perspectives are deliciously wrong. All the objects on the table are painted as in a primitive Last Supper.

PERLIMPLÍN. Then you will do as I say?

MARCOLFA, *crying.* Don't worry, master.

PERLIMPLÍN. Marcolfa, why do you keep on crying?

MARCOLFA. Your Grace knows. On your wedding night five men entered your bedroom through the balconies. Five! Representatives of the five races of the earth. The European, with his beard—the Indian—the Negro—the Yellow Man—and the American. And you unaware of it all.

PERLIMPLÍN. That is of no importance.

MARCOLFA. Just imagine: yesterday I saw her with another one.

PERLIMPLÍN, *intrigued.* Really?

MARCOLFA. And she didn't even hide from me.

PERLIMPLÍN. But I am happy, Marcolfa.

MARCOLFA. The master astonishes me.

PERLIMPLÍN. You have no idea how happy I am. I have learned many things and above all I can imagine many others.

MARCOLFA. My master loves her too much.

PERLIMPLÍN. Not as much as she deserves.

MARCOLFA. Here she comes.

PERLIMPLÍN. Please leave.

Marcolfa leaves and Perlimplín hides in a corner. Enter Belisa dressed in a red dress of eighteenth-century style. The skirt, at the back, is slit, allowing silk stockings to be seen. She wears huge earrings and a red hat trimmed with big ostrich plumes.

BELISA. Again I have failed to see him. In my walk through the park they were all behind me except him. His skin must be dark, and his kisses must perfume and burn at the same time—like saffron and cloves. Sometimes he passes underneath my balconies and moves his hand slowly in a greeting that makes my breasts tremble.

PERLIMPLÍN. Ahem!

BELISA, *turning*. Oh! What a fright you gave me.

PERLIMPLÍN, *approaching her affectionately*. I observe you were speaking to yourself.

BELISA, *distastefully*. Go away!

PERLIMPLÍN. Shall we take a walk?

BELISA. No.

PERLIMPLÍN. Shall we go to the confectioner's?

BELISA. I said no!

PERLIMPLÍN. Pardon.

A letter rolled about a stone falls through the balcony. Perlimplín picks it up.

BELISA. Give that to me.

PERLIMPLÍN. Why?

BELISA. Because it's for me.

PERLIMPLÍN, *jokingly*. And who told you that?

BELISA. Perlimplín! Don't read it!

PERLIMPLÍN, *jokingly severe*. What are you trying to say?

BELISA, *weeping*. Give me that letter!

PERLIMPLÍN, *approaching her*. Poor Belisa! Because I understand your feelings I give you this paper which means so much to you.

Belisa takes the note and hides it in her bosom.

I can see things. And even though it wounds me deeply, I understand you live in a drama.

BELISA, *tenderly*. Perlimplín!

PERLIMPLÍN. I know that you are faithful to me, and that you will continue to be so.

BELISA, *fondly.* I've never known any man other than my Perlimplinillo.

PERLIMPLÍN. That's why I want to help you as any good husband should when his wife is a model of virtue. . . . Look.

He closes the door and adopts a mysterious air.

I know everything! I realized immediately. You are young and I am old . . . what can we do about it! But I understand perfectly.

Pause. In a low voice.

Has he come by here today?

BELISA. Twice.

PERLIMPLÍN. And has he signaled to you?

BELISA. Yes . . . but in a manner that's a little disdainful . . . and that hurts me!

PERLIMPLÍN. Don't be afraid. Two weeks ago I saw that young man for the first time. I can tell you with all sincerity that his beauty dazzled me. I have never seen another man in whom manliness and delicacy meet in a more harmonious fashion. Without knowing why, I thought of you.

BELISA. I haven't seen his face . . . but . . .

PERLIMPLÍN. Don't be afraid to speak to me. I know you love him . . . and I love you now as if I were your father. I am far from that foolishness; therefore . . .

BELISA. He writes me letters.

PERLIMPLÍN. I know that.

BELISA. But he doesn't let me see him.

PERLIMPLÍN. That's strange.

BELISA. And it even seems . . . as though he scorns me.

PERLIMPLÍN. How innocent you are!

BELISA. But there's no doubt he loves me as I wish. . . .

PERLIMPLÍN, *intrigued.* How is that?

BELISA. The letters I have received from other men . . . and which I didn't answer because I had my little husband, spoke to me of ideal lands—of dreams and wounded hearts. But these letters from him . . . they . . .

PERLIMPLÍN. Speak without fear.

BELISA. They speak about me . . . about my body . . .

PERLIMPLÍN, *stroking her hair*. About your body!

BELISA. "What do I want your soul for?" he tells me. "The soul is the patrimony of the weak, of crippled heroes and sickly people. Beautiful souls are at death's door, leaning upon whitest hairs and lean hands. Belisa, it is not your soul that I desire, but your white and soft trembling body."

PERLIMPLÍN. Who could that beautiful youth be?

BELISA. No one knows.

PERLIMPLÍN, *inquisitive*. No one?

BELISA. I have asked all my friends.

PERLIMPLÍN, *inscrutably and decisively*. And if I should tell you I know him?

BELISA. Is that possible?

PERLIMPLÍN. Wait.

Goes to the balcony.

Here he is.

BELISA, *running*. Yes?

PERLIMPLÍN. He has just turned the corner.

BELISA, *choked*. Oh!

PERLIMPLÍN. Since I am an old man, I want to sacrifice myself for you. This that I do no one ever did before. But I am already beyond the world and the ridiculous morals of its people. Good-by.

BELISA. Where are you going?

PERLIMPLÍN, *at the door, grandiosely*. Later you will know everything. Later.

CURTAIN

SCENE 3

A grove of cypresses and orange trees. When the curtain rises, Marcolfa and Perlimplín appear in the garden.

MARCOLFA. Is it time yet?

PERLIMPLÍN. No, it isn't time yet.

MARCOLFA. But what has my master thought?

PERLIMPLÍN. Everything he hadn't thought before.

MARCOLFA, *weeping.* It's my fault!

PERLIMPLÍN. Oh, if you only knew what gratitude there is in my heart for you!

MARCOLFA. Before this, everything went smoothly. In the morning, I would take my master his coffee and milk and grapes. . . .

PERLIMPLÍN. Yes . . . the grapes! The grapes! But . . . I? It seems to me that a hundred years have passed. Before, I could not think of the extraordinary things the world holds. I was merely on the threshold. On the other hand . . . today! Belisa's love has given me a precious wealth that I ignored before . . . don't you see? Now I can close my eyes and . . . I can see what I want. For example, my mother, when she was visited by the elves. Oh, you know how elves are . . . tiny. It's marvelous! They can dance upon my little finger.

MARCOLFA. Yes, yes, the elves, the elves, but . . . how about this other?

PERLIMPLÍN. The other? Ah!

With satisfaction.

What did you tell my wife?

MARCOLFA. Even though I'm not very good at these things, I told her what the master had instructed me to say . . . that that young man . . . would come tonight at ten o'clock sharp to the garden, wrapped, as usual, in his red cape.

PERLIMPLÍN. And she?

MARCOLFA. She became as red as a geranium, put her hands to her heart, and kissed her lovely braids passionately.

PERLIMPLÍN, *enthusiastic.* So she got red as a geranium, eh? And, what did she say?

MARCOLFA. She just sighed; that's all. But, oh! such a sigh!

PERLIMPLÍN. Oh, yes! As no woman ever sighed before! Isn't that so?

MARCOLFA. Her love must border on madness.

PERLIMPLÍN, *vibrantly.* That's it! What I need is for her to love that youth more than her own body. And there is no doubt that she loves him.

MARCOLFA, *weeping.* It frightens me to hear you . . . but how is it possible? Don Perlimplín, how is it possible that you yourself should encourage your wife in the worst of sins?

PERLIMPLÍN. Because Perlimplín has no honor and wants to amuse himself! Now do you see? Tonight the new and unknown lover of my lady Belisa will come. What should I do but sing?

Singing.

Don Perlimplín has no honor! Has no honor!

MARCOLFA. Let my master know that from this moment on I consider myself dismissed from his service. We servants also have a sense of shame.

PERLIMPLÍN. Oh, innocent Marcolfa! Tomorrow you will be as free as a bird. Wait until tomorrow. Now go and perform your duty. You will do what I have told you?

MARCOLFA, *leaving, drying her tears.* What else is there for me to do? What else?

PERLIMPLÍN. Good, that's how I like it.

A sweet serenade begins to sound. Don Perlimplín hides behind some rosebushes.

VOICES.

> Upon the banks of the river
> the passing night has paused to bathe.
> The passing night has paused to bathe.
> And on the breasts of Belisa
> the flowers languish of their love.
> The flowers languish of their love.

PERLIMPLÍN.

> The flowers languish of their love.

VOICES.

> The naked night stands there singing,
> singing on the bridge of March.
> Singing on the bridge of March.
> Belisa, too, bathes her body
> with briny water and spikenard.
> With briny water and spikenard.

PERLIMPLÍN.

> The flowers languish of their love!

VOICES.

> The night of anise and silver
> on all the roofs glows and shines.
> On all the roofs glows and shines.
> The silver of streams and of mirrors
> and anise white of your thighs.
> And anise white of your thighs.

PERLIMPLÍN. The flowers languish of their love!

Belisa appears in the garden splendidly dressed. The moon lights the stage.

BELISA. What voices fill with sweet harmony the air of this fragment of the night? I have felt your warmth and your weight, delicious youth of my soul. Oh! The branches are moving . . .

A man dressed in a red cape appears and crosses the garden cautiously.

BELISA. Sh! Here! Here!

The man signals with his hand that he will return immediately.

Oh! Yes . . . come back my love! Like a jasmine floating and without roots, the sky will fall over my moistening shoulders. Night! My night of mint and lapis lazuli . . .

Perlimplín appears.

PERLIMPLÍN, *surprised.* What are you doing here?

BELISA. I was walking.

PERLIMPLÍN. Only that?

BELISA. In the clear night.

PERLIMPLÍN, *severely.* What were you doing here?

BELISA, *surprised.* Don't you know?

PERLIMPLÍN. I don't know anything.

BELISA. You sent me the message.

PERLIMPLÍN, *with ardent desire.* Belisa . . . are you still waiting for him?

BELISA. With more ardor than ever.

PERLIMPLÍN, *severely.* Why?

BELISA. Because I love him.

PERLIMPLÍN. Well, he will come.

BELISA. The perfume of his flesh passes beyond his clothes. I love him! Perlimplín, I love him! It seems to me that I am another woman!

PERLIMPLÍN. That is my triumph.

BELISA. What triumph?

PERLIMPLÍN. The triumph of my imagination.

BELISA. It's true that you helped me love him.

PERLIMPLÍN. As now I will help you mourn him.

BELISA, *puzzled.* Perlimplín! What are you saying?

The clock sounds ten. A nightingale sings.

PERLIMPLÍN. It is the hour.

BELISA. He should be here this instant.

PERLIMPLÍN. He's leaping the walls of my garden.

BELISA. Wrapped in his red cape.

PERLIMPLÍN, *drawing a dagger*. Red as his blood.

BELISA, *holding him*. What are you going to do?

PERLIMPLÍN, *embracing her*. Belisa, do you love him?

BELISA, *forcefully*. Yes!

PERLIMPLÍN. Well, since you love him so much, I don't want him ever to leave you. And in order that he should be completely yours, it has come to me that the best thing would be to stick this dagger in his gallant heart. Would you like that?

BELISA. For God's sake, Perlimplín!

PERLIMPLÍN. Then, dead, you will be able to caress him in your bed—so handsome and well groomed—without the fear that he should cease to love you. He will love you with the infinite love of the dead, and I will be free of this dark little nightmare of your magnificent body.

Embracing her.

Your body . . . that I will never decipher!

Looking into the garden.

Look where he comes. Let go, Belisa. Let go!

He exits running.

BELISA, *desperately*. Marcolfa! Bring me the sword from the dining room; I am going to run my husband's throat through.

Calling.

> Don Perlimplín
> Evil husband!
> If you kill him,
> I'll kill you!

A man wrapped in a large red cape appears among the branches. He is wounded and stumbling.

BELISA. My love! . . . Who has wounded you in the breast?

The man hides his face in his cape. The cape must be enormous and cover him to the feet. She embraces him.

Who opened your veins so that you fill my garden with blood? Love, let me look at your face for an instant. Oh! Who has killed you . . . Who?

PERLIMPLÍN, *uncovering himself.* Your husband has just killed me with this emerald dagger.

He shows the dagger stuck in his chest.

BELISA, *frightened.* Perlimplín!

PERLIMPLÍN. He ran away through the fields and you will never see him again. He killed me because he knew I loved you as no one else. . . . While he wounded me he shouted: "Belisa has a soul now!" Come near.

He has stretched out on the bench.

BELISA. Why is this? And you are truly wounded.

PERLIMPLÍN. Perlimplín killed me. . . . Ah, Don Perlimplín! Youngish old man, manikin without strength, you couldn't enjoy the body of Belisa . . . the body of Belisa was for younger muscles and warm lips. . . . I, on the other hand, loved your body only . . . your body! But he has killed me . . . with this glowing branch of precious stones.

BELISA. What have you done?

PERLIMPLÍN, *near death.* Don't you understand? I am my soul and you are your body. Allow me this last moment, since you have loved me so much, to die embracing it.

Belisa, half naked, draws near and embraces him.

BELISA. Yes . . . but the young man? Why have you deceived me?

PERLIMPLÍN. The young man?

Closes his eyes. The stage is left in magical light. Marcolfa enters.

MARCOLFA. Madam . . .

BELISA, *weeping.* Don Perlimplín is dead!

MARCOLFA. I knew it! Now his shroud will be the youthful red suit in which he used to walk under his own balconies.

BELISA, *weeping.* I never thought he was so devious.

MARCOLFA. You have found out too late. I shall make him a crown of flowers like the noonday sun.

BELISA, *confused, as if in another world.* Perlimplín, what have you done, Perlimplín?

MARCOLFA. Belisa, now you are another woman. You are dressed in the most glorious blood of my master.

BELISA. But who was this man? Who was he?

MARCOLFA. The beautiful adolescent whose face you never will see.

BELISA. Yes, yes, Marcolfa—I love him—I love him with all the strength of my flesh and my soul—but where is the young man in the red cape? Dear God, where is he?

MARCOLFA. Don Perlimplín, sleep peacefully. . . . Do you hear? Don Perlimplín. . . . Do you hear her?

The bells sound.

CURTAIN

DOÑA ROSITA, THE SPINSTER
OR
THE LANGUAGE OF THE FLOWERS

A POEM OF 1900 GRANADA,
DIVIDED INTO VARIOUS GARDENS,
WITH SCENES OF SONG AND DANCE

(1935)

CHARACTERS

DOÑA ROSITA

THE HOUSEKEEPER

THE AUNT

FIRST MANOLA

SECOND MANOLA

THIRD MANOLA

FIRST SPINSTER

SECOND SPINSTER

THIRD SPINSTER

THE MOTHER OF THE SPINSTERS

FIRST MISS AYOLA

SECOND MISS AYOLA

THE UNCLE

THE NEPHEW

INSTRUCTOR OF POLITICAL ECONOMY

DON MARTÍN

MR. X

THE YOUTH

TWO WORKMEN

A VOICE

ACT ONE

A room leading to a greenhouse.

UNCLE. And my seeds?

HOUSEKEEPER. They were here.

UNCLE. Well, they're not now.

AUNT. Hellebore, fuchsias and the chrysanthemums, vio-laceous Louis Passy, and silver-white altair with heliotrope points.

UNCLE. You must be careful of the flowers.

HOUSEKEEPER. If you say that because of me . . .

AUNT. Quiet. Don't talk back.

UNCLE. I say that because of everybody. Yesterday I found the dahlia tubers trampled underfoot.

Enters the greenhouse.

You do not appreciate my greenhouse; since 1807, the year in which the Countess of Wandes was able to raise a musk rose, no one in Granada has been able to raise one but me —not even the university botanist. You must have more respect for my plants.

HOUSEKEEPER. Oh, so I don't respect them?

AUNT. Hush! You're the worst.

HOUSEKEEPER. Yes, madam. But I am not the one who says that from so much watering of the flowers and so much water everywhere, toads are going to appear in the sofa.

AUNT. You certainly enjoy smelling them at times.

HOUSEKEEPER. No, madam. To me flowers smell like a child's funeral, a nun's taking holy vows, or a church altar. Of sad things. Where there is an orange or a good quince, let the roses of the world go by. But here . . . roses to the right, basil to the left, anemones, sage, petunias, and those new fashionable flowers, the chrysanthemums, tousle-headed like gypsy girls. How I long to see planted in this garden a pear tree, a cherry tree, or a persimmon!

AUNT. So you could eat them!

HOUSEKEEPER. That's what I have a mouth for . . . as they used to say in my village:

> The mouth is useful when we eat,
> The legs are useful when we dance,
> And women have a thing quite neat . . .

She stops, goes to the Aunt, and whispers.

AUNT. Heavens!

Crosses herself.

HOUSEKEEPER. Those are rustic obscenities.

Crosses herself.

ROSITA, *enters rapidly. She is dressed in rose, in the style of 1900: leg-of-mutton sleeves and braid trimming.* And my hat? Where is my hat? The bells have rung thirty times at San Luis!

HOUSEKEEPER. I left it on the table.

ROSITA. Well, it isn't there.

They search. The Housekeeper leaves.

AUNT. Have you looked in the clothespress?

The Aunt leaves.

HOUSEKEEPER, *enters.* I cannot find it.

ROSITA. Can it be possible that no one knows where my hat is?

HOUSEKEEPER. Wear the blue one with the daisies.

ROSITA. You're crazy.

HOUSEKEEPER. Then you're crazier.

AUNT, *re-enters.* Come, here it is!

Rosita takes it and goes running out.

HOUSEKEEPER. She wants everything in such a hurry. She wishes that today were day after tomorrow. She starts flying and slips through our hands. When she was a child, I used to have to tell her every day the story of when she should

be an old lady: "My Rosita is now eighty years old . . ."
always something like that. When have you ever seen her
sit down to tat or make frivolité or garland points or drawn
work to decorate a cap?

AUNT. Never.

HOUSEKEEPER. Always from shout to sheet and sheet to
shout, from shout to sheet and sheet to shout!

AUNT. Watch your tongue!

HOUSEKEEPER. If I make a slip of the tongue, it would not
be a word new to you.

AUNT. It's true that I've never liked to say no to her: who
wants to grieve a child who has no father or mother?

HOUSEKEEPER. Neither father nor mother nor a little dog
to bark for her, but she does have an uncle and aunt worth
a treasure.

Embraces her.

UNCLE, *within.* This is really too much!

AUNT. Holy Mother!

UNCLE. It's all very well for the tubers to be trampled,
but it's simply unbearable for the rosebush I most cherish
to have its little leaves broken. I think more of it than of
the musk rose, or the hispid, the pompon, or the damask
rose, or even Queen Elizabeth's eglantine.

To the Aunt.

Come in here; just come in here and you will see.

AUNT. Is it torn?

UNCLE. No, nothing very serious happened to it, but it
could have.

HOUSEKEEPER. We'll never hear the end of it!

UNCLE. I ask myself: who turned over the flowerpot?

HOUSEKEEPER. Don't you look at me.

UNCLE. Then was it I?

HOUSEKEEPER. Are there no cats or dogs, or a sudden
gust of wind to blow through the window?

AUNT. Silence now: go sweep the greenhouse.

HOUSEKEEPER. It's easy to see that in this house one is not permitted to speak.

UNCLE, *enters.* It's a rose you have never seen: a surprise I prepared for you. It's unbelievable. The rosa declinata with its drooping buds, and the inermis without thorns—a marvel isn't it? Not a thorn! . . . and the myrtifolia which comes from Belgium, and the sulfurata, which blooms in the darkness. But this one surpasses them all in rarity. The botanists call it Rosa Mutabile; that is to say: it changes. . . . This book has its description and its picture; look! It is red in the morning—

Opens the book.

—in the evening it changes to white, and at night it shatters.

>   She opens in the morning
>   red as blood.
>   The dew dare not touch her
>   for it would burn.
>   At noon, full-blown,
>   she is hard as coral.
>   Even the sun at the window
>   looks in to see her glow.
>   When the birds begin
>   to sing among the branches,
>   and the afternoon faints
>   on the violets of the sea,
>   she turns pale, with the pallor
>   of a cheek of salt.
>   And when night is blown
>   on a soft metallic horn,
>   while the stars advance,
>   while the winds retreat,
>   on the very edge of darkness
>   her petals begin to rain.

AUNT. And has it a bud yet?

UNCLE. One that is just beginning to open.

AUNT. Does it last only one day?

UNCLE. Only one. But I intend to pass all that day by its side to see how it changes white.

ROSITA, *entering*. My parasol.

UNCLE. Her parasol.

AUNT, *shouting*. The parasol!

HOUSEKEEPER, *appearing*. Here's the parasol!

Rosita takes the parasol and kisses her Aunt and Uncle.

ROSITA. How do I look?

UNCLE. A beauty!

AUNT. Not another like you.

ROSITA, *opening the parasol*. And now?

HOUSEKEEPER. Heavens! Close the parasol! It shouldn't be opened in the house! It's bad luck!
> By the wheel of Saint Bartholomew
> and Saint Joseph's staff that grew,
> by the holy laurel too,
> enemy, retreat and rue
> Jerusalem's four corners through.

All laugh. The Uncle leaves.

ROSITA, *closing the parasol*. There, then!

HOUSEKEEPER. Never do that again . . . ji-miny!

ROSITA. Goodness!

AUNT. What were you going to say?

HOUSEKEEPER. Well, I didn't really say it!

ROSITA. Until later!

Exits laughingly.

AUNT. Who is going with you?

ROSITA, *looking in*. I'm going with the Manolas.*

HOUSEKEEPER. And with your sweetheart.

AUNT. Her sweetheart, I think, was busy.

---

* *Manola:* the high-spirited young coquette, conscious of her charms, and able to accentuate them through the witchery lent by flowers, high combs, a lace mantilla, or a fan—and usually all of these. We have come to think of the *Manola* as typically Spanish, and, indeed, she has always existed. In Goya's day she was called the *Maja*.

HOUSEKEEPER. I don't know which one I like better: her sweetheart, or her.

The Aunt sits down to make lace with bobbins.

A pair of cousins fit to put in a showcase! And if they should die, heaven forbid, embalm them and put them in a niche of crystals and snow. Which one do you like most?

She starts dusting.

AUNT. Both. I love them as niece and nephew.

HOUSEKEEPER. One for the upper sheet and one for the lower sheet, but . . .

AUNT. Rosita grew up with me . . .

HOUSEKEEPER. Naturally. And I don't believe in blood ties. This is what I think. The blood runs down in the veins, but you can't see it. So one loves a second cousin more that one sees every day, than a brother who is far away. And the reason is this: . . .

AUNT. Get on with your cleaning, woman.

HOUSEKEEPER. Right away. Here one isn't allowed to even open her mouth. You raise a beautiful little girl for this. Abandon your own children in a hut, trembling with hunger.

AUNT. You mean with cold.

HOUSEKEEPER. Trembling with everything. Just to be told —shut up! And, as I'm a servant, there's nothing to do but shut up. So I do that and don't dare answer back and say . . .

AUNT. And say what?

HOUSEKEEPER. And say—drop those bobbins with all that clicking. My head is going to burst with that clicking.

AUNT, *laughing.* Go see who's calling.

The stage is silent and only the clicking of the bobbins is heard.

PEDDLER'S VOICE. Ca-a-amo-o-mile, fine ca-a-amomile from the mou-mountains!

AUNT, *talking to herself.* We should buy some more camomile. There are occasions when one needs it. . . . The next time he comes . . . thirty-seven, thirty-eight . . .

PEDDLER'S VOICE, *distantly.* Ca-a-amo-o-mile, fine ca-a-amomile from the mountains!

AUNT, *placing a pin.* And forty.

NEPHEW, *entering.* Aunt . . .

AUNT, *without looking at him.* Hello. Sit down if you like. Rosita has already left.

NEPHEW. With whom did she go?

AUNT. With the Manolas.

Pauses, looks at Nephew.

Something has happened to you.

NEPHEW. Yes.

AUNT, *disturbed.* I can almost guess what. I hope I'm wrong.

NEPHEW. No. Read this.

AUNT, *reads.* Well, this is only what was to be expected. That's why I opposed your engagement with Rosita. I knew that sooner or later you would have to go to your parents. And quite nearby, too! It's a forty days' journey to Tucumán. If I were a man and young I'd slap your face. . . .

NEPHEW. It's not my fault I'm in love with my cousin. Do you imagine I like this? It's precisely because I want to stay that I have come here.

AUNT. Stay? Stay? Your duty is to go. The hacienda is many miles wide and your father is old. I'm the one who must force you to take the boat. But you will embitter my life. I don't even want to think of your cousin. You are going to shoot an arrow with purple* ribbons in her heart. Now she'll find out that linen isn't merely to embroider flowers on, but also to dry tears.

NEPHEW. What do you advise me to do?

---

* Color associated with suffering and sadness.

AUNT. To go. Remember that your father is my brother. Here you are only a walker in little gardens—and there you will be a workingman.

NEPHEW. But I should like to . . .

AUNT. Get married? Are you crazy? Only when your future is assured. And take Rosita with you, no? Only over my dead body and your uncle's.

NEPHEW. I was just talking. I know very well that I cannot. But I want Rosita to wait for me because I'll be back soon.

AUNT. If you don't take up with a Tucumán girl first. I should have bitten my tongue off before I consented to your engagement; because my child will be left alone within these four walls and you will go free across the ocean, across those rivers, through those citron groves, and my little girl here, one day just like another, and you over there, with your horse and musket shooting pheasants.

NEPHEW. There's no reason for you to talk to me in that fashion. I gave my word and I will keep it. In order to keep his word my father is in America and you know . . .

AUNT, *softly.* Quiet.

NEPHEW. I'll be quiet, but don't you confuse respect with lack of honor.

AUNT, *with Andalusian irony.* Pardon! Pardon! I had forgotten you were a man now.

HOUSEKEEPER, *enters weeping.* If he were a man he wouldn't go.

AUNT, *sternly.* Silence!

The Housekeeper weeps with great sobs.

NEPHEW. I will be back in a minute. Please tell her.

AUNT. Never mind. The old people are the ones who have to bear the hard times.

The Nephew leaves.

HOUSEKEEPER. Oh, what a pity about my little girl! What a pity! What a pity! These are the men of today! Even if I

had to beg in the streets I would stay by the side of this
prize. Once more tears will come to the house. Oh, Madam!

Recovering.

I hope the sea serpent eats him!

AUNT. God will decide that!

HOUSEKEEPER.

> By the sesame seed,
> By the three holy questions
> And the cinnamon flower,
> May he have bad nights
> And bad seeding times.
> By the well of St. Nicholas
> May his salt turn to poison.

She takes a water jar and makes a cross on the ground.

AUNT. Don't curse. Go to your work.

Housekeeper leaves. Laughter is heard. The Aunt leaves.

FIRST MANOLA, *entering and closing her parasol.* Ay!

SECOND MANOLA, *likewise.* Ay, what coolness.

THIRD MANOLA, *likewise.* Ay!

ROSITA, *likewise.*

> For whom are the sighs,
> Of my three lovely Manolas?

FIRST MANOLA.

> For no one.

SECOND MANOLA.

> For the wind.

THIRD MANOLA.

> For a gallant who courts me.

ROSITA.

> What hands will gather
> The sighs from your lips?

FIRST MANOLA.

> The wall.

SECOND MANOLA.
>A certain picture.

THIRD MANOLA.
>The hemstitch of my pillow.

ROSITA.
>I too want to sigh.
>Ay, friends! Ay, Manolas!

FIRST MANOLA.
>Who will reap them?

ROSITA.
>   Two eyes
>That make the shadow white,
>Whose brows are vines
>Where daybreak sleeps.
>And, though black, they are
>Two evenings with poppies.

FIRST MANOLA.
>Bind a ribbon round that sigh!

SECOND MANOLA.
>Ay!

THIRD MANOLA.
>Lucky you!

FIRST MANOLA.
>Lucky!

ROSITA.
>Don't mislead me, for I know
>Certain rumors about you.

FIRST MANOLA.
>Rumors are like charlock.

SECOND MANOLA.
>Like refrains of waves.

ROSITA.
>Let me tell you . . .

FIRST MANOLA.
>Begin!

THIRD MANOLA.

> Rumors are like crowns.

ROSITA.

> Granada, Elvira Street,
> where the manolas live,
> who go to the Alhambra
> in threes and fours, alone.
> One is dressed in green,
> the other in mauve, the third
> wears a Scotch bodice
> with ribbons to the train.
> The two in front are herons,
> the one behind, a dove;
> along the poplar lane
> they open mysterious muslins.
> Ay, how dark is the Alhambra!
> Where will the Manolas go
> while the fountain and the rose
> suffer in the shade?
> Which lovers will expect them?
> Under which myrtle will they rest?
> Whose hands will steal the perfume
> from their two round flowers?
> No one goes with them, no one;
> two herons and a dove.
> But there are gallants in the world
> who hide behind leaves.
> The cathedral has left
> bronzes which the breeze takes up.
> The Genil sleeps his oxen,
> and the Dauro his butterflies.
> The night arrives laden
> with its hills of shadow;
> one shows her shoes
> between the silk lace flounces,
> the older opens wide her eyes,
> and the younger half-closes hers.
> Who will they be, those three,
> with high breasts and long trains?

Why do they wave their handkerchiefs?
Where will they go at these hours?
Granada, Elvira Street,
where the Manolas live,
who go to the Alhambra,
in threes and fours, alone.

FIRST MANOLA.
Let the rumor spread
its waves over Granada.

SECOND MANOLA.
Have we a sweetheart?

ROSITA.
None of you.

SECOND MANOLA.
Did I tell the truth?

ROSITA.
Completely.

THIRD MANOLA.
White frost laces trim
our bridal clothes.

ROSITA.
But . . .

FIRST MANOLA.
We like the night.

ROSITA.
But . . .

SECOND MANOLA.
Through darkened streets

FIRST MANOLA.
we go up to the Alhambra,
in threes and fours, alone.

THIRD MANOLA.
Ay!

SECOND MANOLA.
Hush!

THIRD MANOLA.
> Why?

SECOND MANOLA.
> Ay!

FIRST MANOLA.
> Ay, let no one hear it.

ROSITA.
> Alhambra, jasmine of sorrow,
> where the moon reposes.

HOUSEKEEPER, *very sadly.* Child, your aunt is calling you.

ROSITA. Have you been crying?

HOUSEKEEPER, *controlling herself.* No . . . it's just that
. . . something . . .

ROSITA. Don't frighten me. What has happened.

She leaves quickly, looking toward the Housekeeper. When Rosita leaves, the Housekeeper begins to cry silently.

FIRST MANOLA, *loudly.* What is the matter?

SECOND MANOLA. Tell us.

HOUSEKEEPER. Hush.

THIRD MANOLA, *in a low voice.* Bad news?

The Housekeeper takes them to the door and looks out to where Rosita went.

HOUSEKEEPER. She is telling her now!

Pause, while all listen.

FIRST MANOLA. Rosita is crying. Let's go in.

HOUSEKEEPER. Come and I'll tell you about it. Leave her alone! You can go out through the side gate.

They leave. The stage is empty. A very distant piano plays a Czerny étude. Pause. The Nephew enters and on reaching the center of the room stops because Rosita enters. The two stand regarding each other face to face. The Nephew advances. He takes her by the waist. She leans her head on his shoulder.

ROSITA.

    Why were your treacherous eyes
    welded to my own?
    And why did your hands weave
    flowers over my head?
    Only a nightingale's grieving
    do you leave to my youth;
    after steering my love's course
    to your form and presence,
    you break by your cruel absence
    the strings of my lute.

NEPHEW, *takes her to a "vis-à-vis" and they sit down.*

    Oh, cousin, who are my treasure,
    Nightingale in winter snow,
    your mouth must be firm closed
    against imagined cold;
    my departure is not of ice,
    for though I cross the sea,
    the water must lend to me
    gardenias of foam and quiet
    that I may contain my fire
    when I should fear to burn.

ROSITA.

    While dozing one night
    on my jasmine balcony
    I saw two cherubs descend
    to an enamored rose;
    bright scarlet she became
    though she had first been white;
    but like a tender flower,
    her petals all afire,
    wounded, began to fall,
    by the first kiss of love.
    Thus, I, innocent cousin,
    within my myrtle garden,
    gave the wind my longing,
    my whiteness to the fountain.
    Tender thoughtless gazelle,
    I raised my eyes and saw you,

and felt my heart pierced
by trembling needles
and open wounds in me
red as the gillyflower.

NEPHEW.

I must return, my cousin,
to take you by my side
in burnished golden ship
with sails of happiness;
light and shade, night and day,
I'll think only of loving you.

ROSITA.

But the poison that overflows,
love, on a soul alone,
will weave with land and wave
the garments of my death.

NEPHEW.

When my stallion slow
eats grasses wet with dew,
when the river's fog
whitens the wall of wind;
when the violent summer
with scarlet paints the plain
and frost leaves in me
bright needles from a star,
I tell you, because I love you,
that I will die for you.

ROSITA.

I long to see you come
some evening through Granada
when all the light's besalted,
nostalgic for the sea;
a yellow lemon grove,
a white-bled jasmine garden,
entangled by the stones
that will impede your way,
and nards like whirlpools
that make insane my roof.
Will you return?

NEPHEW.

> Yes. I'll return!

ROSITA.

> And what refulgent dove
> announces your arrival?

NEPHEW.

> The dove that is my faith.

ROSITA.

> Then see, I will embroider
> white sheets for both of us.

NEPHEW.

> By the diamonds of the Lord,
> and his side's carnation,
> I swear I will return.

ROSITA.

> Good-by, cousin!

NEPHEW.

> Cousin, good-by!

They embrace in the "vis-à-vis." The piano is heard distantly. The Nephew leaves. Rosita is left weeping. The Uncle appears and crosses the stage toward the greenhouse. When she sees her uncle, Rosita picks up the rose book which is near her hand.

UNCLE. What were you doing?

ROSITA. Nothing.

UNCLE. Were you reading?

ROSITA. Yes.

The Uncle leaves.

ROSITA, *reads.*

> She opens in the morning
> red as blood.
> The dew dare not touch her
> for it would burn.
> At noon, full-blown,
> she is hard as coral.

Even the sun at the window
looks in to see her glow.
When the birds begin
to sing among the branches,
and the afternoon faints
on the violets of the sea,
she turns pale, with the pallor
of a cheek of salt.
And when night is blown
on a soft metallic horn,
while the stars advance,
while the winds retreat,
on the very edge of darkness
her petals begin to rain.

CURTAIN

ACT TWO

A room of Doña Rosita's house. The garden in the background.

MR. X. Therefore, I always will be of this century.

UNCLE. The century we have just begun will be a century of materialism.

MR. X. But of much more progress than the one which just passed. My friend, Mr. Longoria, of Madrid, has just bought an automobile with which he can hurl himself along at the fantastic speed of eighteen miles per hour; and the Shah of Persia, who certainly is a most pleasant man, has also bought a Panhard Levasson motor car of twenty-four horsepower.

UNCLE. And I say: where are they going in such a great hurry? Just see what happened in the Paris-Madrid race, which had to be suspended because before they reached Bordeaux all the racers killed themselves.

MR. X. Count Zboronsky, dead in that accident, and Marcel Renault, or Renol, since in both fashions it is wont to be and can be pronounced, dead also in that accident, are martyrs of science who will be enshrined the day a religion of the positive comes. Renault I knew quite well. Poor Marcello.

UNCLE. You will not convince me.

He sits.

MR. X, *one foot on the chair, playing with his cane.* Superlatively! Although a professor of political economy cannot argue with a cultivator of roses. But in this day and age, believe me, neither quietisms nor obscurantist ideas can prevail. In this day a road is opened by a Jean-Baptiste Say or Se, since in both fashions it is wont to be and can be pronounced, or a Count Leo Tolstwa, vulgarly

Tolstoy, as elegant in form as he is profound in concept. I feel myself in the living *polis*; I am not in favor of *natura naturata*.

UNCLE. Everyone lives as he can, or as he best knows how in his daily life.

MR. X. That's understood. The earth is a mediocre planet, but one must lend aid to civilization. If Santos Dumont, instead of studying comparative meteorology, had dedicated himself to watching roses, the dirigible aerostat would be in the bosom of Brahma.

UNCLE, *disgusted*. Botany is also a science.

MR. X, *disparagingly*. Yes, but an applied one: to study the juices of the fragrant Anthemis or the rhubarb, or the great Pulsatilla, or the narcotic of the Datura Stramonium.

UNCLE, *innocently*. Do these plants interest you?

MR. X. I do not possess a sufficient volume of experience concerning them. I'm interested in culture, which is different. *Voila!*

Pause.

And Rosita?

UNCLE. Rosita!

Pause. Shouts.

Rosita!

VOICE, *within*. She's not here.

UNCLE. She's not here.

MR. X. I regret it.

UNCLE. I also. Since it is her Saint's day she must have gone to pray the forty credos.

MR. X. Deliver to her for me this pendant. It is a mother-of-pearl Eiffel Tower over two doves which carry in their bills the wheel of industry.

UNCLE. She will be most grateful.

MR. X. I almost brought her a little silver cannon through whose mouth one could see the Virgin of Lourdes, or Lordes, or a buckle for a belt made with a serpent and four dragonflies, but I chose the first as being in better taste.

UNCLE. Thank you.

MR. X. I am charmed with your favorable reception.

UNCLE. Thanks.

MR. X. Place me at the feet of your dear spouse.

UNCLE. Many thanks.

MR. X. Place me at the feet of your enchanting little niece to whom I wish good fortune on the feast day of her Saint.

UNCLE. A thousand thanks.

MR. X. Consider me as your faithful servant.

UNCLE. A million thanks.

MR. X. Once more I repeat . . .

UNCLE. Thank you, thank you, thank you.

MR. X. Then, until always!

He leaves.

UNCLE, *shouting.* Thank you, thank you, thank you!

HOUSEKEEPER, *enters laughing.* I don't know how you have the patience. With that man and with the other—Mr. Confucius Montes de Oca, baptized in lodge number forty-three—the house will burn down some day.

UNCLE. I have told you I don't like you to eavesdrop on our conversations.

HOUSEKEEPER. That is what is called ingratitude. I was behind the door, true enough, but it was not to listen, but to place a broom upside down so that the gentleman would leave.

AUNT, *entering.* Has he left yet?

UNCLE. Yes.

Exits.

HOUSEKEEPER. Is this one also a suitor for Rosita?

AUNT. But why do you speak of suitors? You don't know Rosita!

HOUSEKEEPER. But I do know the suitors.

AUNT. My niece is affianced.

HOUSEKEEPER. Don't make me say it, don't make me say it, don't make me say it.

AUNT. Then be quiet.

HOUSEKEEPER. Does it seem right to you for a man to go away now for fifteen years and leave behind a woman who is the very cream of the crop? She ought to marry. My hands ache from storing away Marseille lace tablecloths and embroidered bed sets and table scarves and gauze bedspreads with raised flowers. It's now she ought to use them and tear them, but she doesn't realize how the time passes. She will have silver hair and still be sewing satin bands on the ruffles of her honeymoon nightgown.

AUNT. But why do you meddle with things that do not concern you?

HOUSEKEEPER, *with surprise*. It's not that I meddle, things meddle with me.

AUNT. I'm sure that she is happy.

HOUSEKEEPER. She just imagines it. Yesterday she had me with her all day at the gate to the circus because she insisted one of the puppeteers resembled her cousin.

AUNT. And did he resemble him really?

HOUSEKEEPER. He was as beautiful as a young priest when he comes to sing his first mass. But your nephew just wishes he had that waist, that white throat, that mustache. They didn't look at all alike. In your family there aren't any good-looking men.

AUNT. Thank you, woman.

HOUSEKEEPER. They are all short and a little stoop-shouldered.

AUNT. Well!

HOUSEKEEPER. That's the real truth, madam. What happened is that Rosita liked the mountebank, just as I liked him and as you would. But she lays it all on the other one. Sometimes I'd like to throw a shoe at her head. Because from so much looking at the sky she's going to get eyes like a cow's.

AUNT. Very well. Now let it rest. It's all right for the clown to speak but not to bark.

HOUSEKEEPER. You won't throw it in my face that I don't love her.

AUNT. Sometimes I think you don't.

HOUSEKEEPER. I would take the bread from my mouth and the blood from my veins if she wanted them.

AUNT, *strongly*. Honey-tongued liar! Words!

HOUSEKEEPER, *strongly*. And deeds! I have proved it, and deeds! I love her more than you.

AUNT. That's a lie.

HOUSEKEEPER, *strongly*. That's the truth!

AUNT. Don't raise your voice to me!

HOUSEKEEPER, *loudly*. That's what I have a tongue for.

AUNT. Be quiet, know-nothing!

HOUSEKEEPER. Forty years at your side.

AUNT, *almost weeping*. You're dismissed!

HOUSEKEEPER, *very loudly*. Thank goodness I won't have to look at you any more!

AUNT, *weeping*. To the street at once!

HOUSEKEEPER, *breaking into tears*. To the street!

She goes weeping toward the door and as she steps outside some object falls. Both are weeping. Pause.

AUNT, *drying her tears, sweetly*. What did you drop?

HOUSEKEEPER, *weeping*. A thermometer case. Louis Quinze style.

AUNT. Yes?

HOUSEKEEPER. Yes, madam.

They weep.

AUNT. May I see it?

HOUSEKEEPER. For Rosita's Saint's day.

She approaches.

AUNT, *sniffling*. It's a precious thing.

HOUSEKEEPER, *in a tearful voice*. In the middle of the velvet there's a fountain made out of real shells. Over the fountain there is a wire arbor with green roses. The water in the basin is a group of blue sequins and the stream of water is the thermometer itself. The puddles around are painted in oil and upon them a nightingale drinks, all embroidered in golden thread. I wanted it to have a spring and wind up and sing, but that could not be.

AUNT. That could not be.

HOUSEKEEPER. But it doesn't need to sing. In the garden we have live ones.

AUNT. That's true.

Pause.

Why have you gone to all this trouble?

HOUSEKEEPER, *crying*. I'd give everything I have for Rosita.

AUNT. You love her as no one else does!

HOUSEKEEPER. But after you.

AUNT. No. You have given her your blood.

HOUSEKEEPER. You have sacrificed your life.

AUNT. But I have done it through duty and you out of generosity.

HOUSEKEEPER, *louder*. Don't you say that!

AUNT. You have proved you love her more than any one.

HOUSEKEEPER. I have done what any one would have done in my case. A servant. You pay me and I serve you.

AUNT. We've always considered you one of the family.

HOUSEKEEPER. A humble servant who gives what she has and nothing more.

AUNT. Why do you say "nothing more"?

HOUSEKEEPER. Well, am I anything else?

AUNT, *irritated*. You can't say that here. I'm going so I won't have to listen to you.

HOUSEKEEPER, *irritated*. Me, too.

They go out quickly, each by a separate door. As the Aunt is going out she runs into the Uncle.

UNCLE. From so much living together, laces seem like thorns to you.

AUNT. It's just that she always wants to have her way.

UNCLE. Don't explain to me. I know it all by heart. . . . Nevertheless, you can't be without her. Yesterday I heard how you explained to her in complete detail about our account at the bank. You don't know how to keep your place. It doesn't seem to me the most suitable topic for conversation with a servant.

AUNT. She's not a servant.

UNCLE, *with sweetness.* Enough, enough. I don't want to contradict you.

AUNT. But can no one even speak with me?

UNCLE. One can, but I prefer to be quiet.

AUNT. Even though those words of reproach are within you.

UNCLE. Why should I say anything at so late a time? To avoid argument, I would make up my bed, clean my suits with soap bark, and change the rugs in my room.

AUNT. It isn't right for you to give yourself this air of a superior man, badly served, when everything in this house is subordinated to your comfort and your likes.

UNCLE, *sweetly.* On the contrary, child.

AUNT. Completely. Instead of making lace, I prune the plants. What do you do for me?

UNCLE. Forgive me. There comes a moment in which people who have lived together many years make a pretext for ill humor and anxiety out of the smallest things, in order to put intensity and worry into what's definitely dead. When we were twenty years old we didn't have any such conversations.

AUNT. No, when we were twenty years old the windows could break . . .

UNCLE. And the cold was a toy in our hands.

Rosita appears. She comes dressed in rose. The styles have changed from the leg-o'-mutton sleeves of 1900. Her skirt is like a bell. She crosses the stage quickly with a pair of scissors in her hand. In the center she pauses.

ROSITA. Has the postman come?

UNCLE. Has he come?

AUNT. I don't know.

Loudly.

Has the postman come?

Pause.

No, not yet.

ROSITA. He always passes at this hour.

UNCLE. He should have been here some time ago.

AUNT. Well, many times he's delayed.

ROSITA. The other day I met him playing hop-scotch with three children and the whole pile of letters on the ground.

AUNT. He'll come.

ROSITA. Let me know.

She goes out quickly.

UNCLE. But where are you going with those scissors?

ROSITA. I'm going to cut some roses.

UNCLE, *astounded.* What? And who has given you permission?

AUNT. I did. Today's her Saint's day.

ROSITA. I want to put some in the jardinière, and in the vase in the front hall.

UNCLE. Every time you cut a rose, it's as if you cut off one of my fingers. I know, it's all the same to you.

Looking at his wife.

I don't want to argue. I know they don't last very long.

The Housekeeper enters.

So says the Waltz of the Roses, which is one of the prettiest compositions of these times, but I cannot restrain the disgust I feel at seeing them in vases.

ROSITA, *to the Housekeeper*. Did the mail come?

HOUSEKEEPER. Well, the only thing roses are good for is to decorate rooms.

ROSITA, *irritated*. I asked you if the mail had come.

HOUSEKEEPER, *irritated*. Do I hide the letters when they come?

AUNT. Go on now and cut the flowers.

ROSITA. There's a drop of bitterness for everything in this house.

HOUSEKEEPER. Yes, we find arsenic in the corners.

Leaves the stage.

AUNT. Are you happy?

ROSITA. I don't know.

AUNT. What does that mean?

ROSITA. When I don't see people I'm happy, but since I have to see them . . .

AUNT. Of course. I don't like the life you lead. Your fiancé doesn't demand that you be a stay-at-home. In his letters he always tells me you should go out.

ROSITA. It's just that in the streets I become aware of how time has passed and I don't want to be disillusioned. They've built another new house in the small plaza. I don't want to find out how time goes.

AUNT. Of course. I have many times advised you to write your cousin and marry someone else here. You're gay and happy. I know there are young fellows and older men in love with you.

ROSITA. But Aunt, my roots are planted very deep, very deep in my feelings. If it were not for seeing people, I could believe that it's just a week since he left. I wait as if it were the first day. Anyway, what is one year, or two, or five?

A little bell sounds.

The mail.

AUNT. I wonder what he sent you?

HOUSEKEEPER, *entering*. Here are those awful old maids.

AUNT. Holy Mary!

ROSITA. Tell them to come in.

HOUSEKEEPER. The mother and the three little girls! Luxury on the outside, but for the mouth, a few stale bread crumbs. A good stiff beating on their. . . . That's what I'd give them. . . .

She leaves. The three awful Girls and their Mother enter. The three Spinsters wear immense hats trimmed with bad feathers, most exaggerated dresses, gloves to the elbow with bracelets over them, and fans hanging from large chains. The Mother wears a faded black dress with a hat of old purple ribbons.

MOTHER. Many happy returns!

They kiss.

ROSITA. Thank you.

Kisses the Spinsters.

Love! Charity! Clemency!

FIRST SPINSTER. Many happy returns.

SECOND SPINSTER. Many happy returns.

THIRD SPINSTER. Many happy returns.

AUNT, *to the Mother*. How are those feet?

MOTHER. Every day worse. If it weren't for these girls, I'd stay at home always.

They sit down.

AUNT. Don't you give yourself the lavender-water treatments?

FIRST SPINSTER. Every night.

SECOND SPINSTER. And the boiled mallows.

AUNT. No rheumatism can resist it.

Pause.

MOTHER. And your husband?

AUNT. He's very well, thank you.

Pause.

MOTHER. With his roses.

AUNT. With his roses.

THIRD SPINSTER. Flowers are so pretty.

SECOND SPINSTER. We have a Saint Francis rosebush in a pot.

ROSITA. But the Saint Francis roses have no odor.

FIRST SPINSTER. Very little.

MOTHER. The ones I like best are the syringas.

THIRD SPINSTER. Violets are also very pretty.

Pause.

MOTHER. Girls, did you bring the card?

THIRD SPINSTER. Yes. It is a little girl in a rose-colored dress, which is, at the same time, a barometer. The monk with his cape is much too common now. According to the humidity, the skirts of the little girl, which are of the finest paper, rise or fall.

ROSITA, *reading.*

> One morning in the field
>   the nightingale's breast
> was full of song that said:
>   "Rosita is the best."

You shouldn't have done it.

AUNT. It's so refined.

MOTHER. I don't lack refinement—what I lack is money.

FIRST SPINSTER. Mamma!

SECOND SPINSTER. Mamma!

THIRD SPINSTER. Mamma!

MOTHER. Now daughters, I'm among friends here. No one can overhear us. But you know very well that since I lost my poor husband I have performed real miracles in order to manage on the pension we have left. I still seem to hear the father of these girls when, generous and gentlemanly as he was, he would say to me: "Henrietta, spend, spend, spend, for I am earning seventy duros now!" But those times are gone. In spite of everything, however, we have kept our position in society. And what anguish I've gone through, madam, so that these daughters could continue wearing hats. How many tears; how many pains for a ribbon or a cluster of curls. Those feathers and those wires have cost me many a sleepless night!

THIRD SPINSTER. Mamma!

MOTHER. That's the truth, my dear child. We daren't in the least exceed our budget. Many times I ask them, "What do you want, my daughters so dear, eggs for breakfast, or chairs at the promenade?" And the three at once answer: "Chairs!"

THIRD SPINSTER. Mother, don't comment further on that. All Granada knows it.

MOTHER. Naturally, what else could they answer? And there we go, eating potatoes or a bunch of grapes, but with a Mongolian cape or a painted parasol or a poplinette blouse with all the trimmings. Because there's nothing else to do. But it's costing me my life, and my eyes fill with tears when I see them competing with those who can do more.

SECOND SPINSTER. Are you going to the park today, Rosita?

ROSITA. No.

THIRD SPINSTER. We always associate there with the Ponce de Leon girls, or with the Herrasti, or the daughters of the Baroness of Saint Matilda of the Papal Benediction. The finest of Granada!

MOTHER. Naturally. They went to Heaven's Gate School together.

Pause.

AUNT, *rising.* Will you have something?

They all rise.

MOTHER. There are no hands like yours for making pine-nut pastry or Heaven Cake.*

FIRST SPINSTER, *to Rosita.* Have you had any news?

---

* *Pastel de gloria,* an Andalusian pastry.

ROSITA. The last letter promised me news. We'll see what this one brings.

THIRD SPINSTER. Have you finished the set with the valencienne lace?

ROSITA. Finished it! I have already made another of nainsook with moiré butterflies.

SECOND SPINSTER. The day you marry you are going to have the best household things in the world.

ROSITA. Alas, I think it all too little. They say that men grow tired of us if they see us always with the same dress.

HOUSEKEEPER, *entering.* Here are those Ayolas, the photographer's daughters.

AUNT. The *Misses* Ayola, you must mean.

HOUSEKEEPER. Here are the high and mighty great ladies of Ayola, photographer to his Majesty, and gold medal at the Madrid Exposition.

Leaves.

AUNT. One must put up with her. But sometimes she sets my nerves on edge.

The Spinsters are with Rosita, looking at some linens.

Servants are impossible.

MOTHER. Cheeky. I have a girl who cleans the flat in the afternoons; she used to earn what they have always earned: one peseta a month and leftovers, which is enough in these times. Well, the other day she flew off the handle saying she wanted five pesetas, and I simply can't afford that.

AUNT. I don't know where it's all going to end.

The Ayola girls enter and greet Rosita gayly. They are richly dressed in the greatly exaggerated style of the period.

ROSITA. Do you know each other?

FIRST AYOLA. By sight.

ROSITA. The Misses Ayola, Mrs. Scarpini and her daughters.

SECOND AYOLA. We've seen them seated on their chairs at the promenade.

They conceal their laughter.

ROSITA. Please be seated.

The Spinsters sit.

AUNT, *to the Ayola girls.* Would you care for some sweets?

SECOND AYOLA. No. We ate just a little while ago. Truly, I ate four eggs with tomato sauce and I was almost unable to rise from the chair.

FIRST AYOLA. How charming!

They laugh. Pause. The Ayolas begin an uncontrollable laughter that communicates itself to Rosita, who tries to stop them. The Spinsters and their Mother are serious. Pause.

AUNT. What children!

MOTHER. Youth.

AUNT. It is the happy age.

ROSITA, *walking around the stage as if arranging things.* Please. Be quiet.

They stop.

AUNT, *to the Third Spinster.* And your piano?

THIRD SPINSTER. I study very little just now. I have so much fancy work to do.

ROSITA. It's a long time since I've heard you.

MOTHER. If it were not for me her fingers would have grown stiff. But I am always there with—Practice! Practice!

SECOND SPINSTER. Since poor Father died she doesn't feel like it. He used to like it so much.

SECOND AYOLA, *with humor.* I remember sometimes his tears would fall.

FIRST SPINSTER. When she played Popper's "Tarantella."

SECOND SPINSTER. And the "Virgin's Prayer."

MOTHER. She had so much soul.

The Ayolas, who have been containing their laughter, burst out now in great peals. Rosita, turning her back to the Spinsters, also laughs, but controls herself.

AUNT. What naughty girls.

FIRST AYOLA. We are laughing because just before we came in here . . .

SECOND AYOLA. This one stumbled and was on the point of turning a somersault . . .

FIRST AYOLA. And I . . .

They laugh. The Spinsters start a slight faint laugh of a weary and sad complexion.

MOTHER. We must go.

AUNT. By no means.

ROSITA, *to all of them*. Well, we are glad you didn't fall. *To the Housekeeper.*

Bring the Saint Kathleen's Bones.

THIRD SPINSTER. They're so rich.

MOTHER. Last year we were given a pound of them.

The Housekeeper comes in with the Bones.

HOUSEKEEPER. Morsels for fine people. *To Rosita.*

The postman is coming through the grove.

ROSITA. Wait for him at the door.

FIRST AYOLA. I don't want to eat. I prefer an anisette.

SECOND AYOLA. And I a brandy.

ROSITA. You've always been a little tippler.

FIRST AYOLA. When I was six years old I used to come here and Rosita's sweetheart got me used to drinking. Don't you remember, Rosita?

ROSITA, *serious*. No.

SECOND AYOLA. Rosita and her sweetheart used to teach me the letters A, B, C. How long ago was that?

AUNT. Fifteen years.

FIRST AYOLA. I almost, almost don't remember your sweetheart's face.

SECOND AYOLA. Didn't he have a scar on his lip?

ROSITA. A scar? Aunt, did he have a scar?

AUNT. Why, child, don't you remember? It was the only thing that detracted a little from his looks.

ROSITA. It wasn't a scar; it was a burn that was a little irritated. Scars are deep.

FIRST AYOLA. Goodness but I want Rosita to get married!

ROSITA. For heaven's sake!

SECOND AYOLA. No more nonsense. So do I!

ROSITA. Why?

FIRST AYOLA. To be in a wedding. As soon as I can, I'm going to get married.

AUNT. Child!

FIRST AYOLA. To anyone—just so I'm not left an old maid.

SECOND AYOLA. I feel the same way.

AUNT, *to the Mother.* What do you think?

FIRST AYOLA. Ah! And if I'm Rosita's friend, it's because she has a sweetheart. Women without sweethearts are faded, overcooked, and all of them . . .

Looks at the Spinsters.

well, not all, but some of them . . . No, all of them have hydrophobia!

AUNT. Here! That's enough of that.

MOTHER. Just let her be.

FIRST SPINSTER. There are many who don't get married because they don't want to.

SECOND AYOLA. I don't believe that.

FIRST SPINSTER, *significantly.* I know it for a fact.

SECOND AYOLA. One who doesn't want to get married quits putting powder on her face and wearing false bosoms and doesn't spend all night and all day at her balcony rail waylaying every passer-by.

SECOND SPINSTER. She may like to take the air.

ROSITA. What a childish discussion!

They laugh strainedly.

AUNT. Well, why don't we play a little?

MOTHER. Go on, child!

THIRD SPINSTER, *rising*. But, what shall I play?

SECOND AYOLA. Play "Viva Frascuelo"!

SECOND SPINSTER. The barcarolle from "The Frigate Numancia."

ROSITA. And why not "What the Flowers Say"?

MOTHER. Oh, yes! "What the Flowers Say"!

To the Aunt.

Have you heard her? She recites and plays at the same time. Precious!

THIRD SPINSTER. I can also recite: "The swallows dark will return, from your balcony their nests to hang."

FIRST AYOLA. That's very sad.

FIRST SPINSTER. Sad things are also beautiful.

AUNT. Come! Come!

THIRD SPINSTER, *at the piano*.
>Mother, take me to the fields,
>in the earliest light of morn,
>there to see the flowers open
>when the branches start to sway.
>One thousand flowers a thousand things
>to as many girls will say,
>and the fountain gossips now
>what the nightingales would not.

ROSITA.
>Already was the rosebud open
>in the earliest light of morn
>so scarlet in its tender blood
>that the dew would not come near;
>so warm it burned upon the stem
>that the breeze itself was seared.
>So tall it was! And how it shone!
>It was open!

THIRD SPINSTER.
>"For you alone my glances are,"
>the heliotrope will always say.

"I will not love you while I live,"
the basil flower is wont to say.
The violet says, "I'm very shy."
"My nature's cold," says the white rose;
the jasmine says, "Have faith in me";
"Impassioned!" the carnation cries.

SECOND SPINSTER.

The hyacinth is bitterness;
the passion flower is for pain.

FIRST SPINSTER.

A mustard flower means disdain;
but lilies ever stand for hope.

AUNT.

Says the gardenia, "I'm your friend";
the passion flower, "I trust in you."
The honeysuckle lulls to sleep;
and evergreen puts you to death.

MOTHER.

Evergreen that stands for death,
flower of the folded hands;
you best exist whene'er the wind
must sadly weep upon your wreath!

ROSITA.

The rose had opened early,
but afternoon was near,
and rumor of sad snow
weighed its branches down;
when darkness returned
when the nightingale sang
she turned pale and lifeless
like one dead from grief;
and when the night a great
metallic horn made sound,
and the winds, subdued,
slept on the mountainside,
she shattered while she sighed
for crystals of the dawn.

THIRD SPINSTER.

> Upon your long soft hair
> the flowers unstemmed must weep,
> some carry tiny knives,
> some water, others fire.

FIRST SPINSTER.

> The flowers have a language
> for maids who are in love.

ROSITA.

> The willow-herb speaks of jealousy;
> the dahlia speaks of shy disdain;
> gardenia is a sigh of love,
> laughter is the fleur-de-lis.
> Yellow flowers all mean hate;
> scarlet flowers stand for fury;
> white ones foretell a wedding
> and blue, a winding sheet.

THIRD SPINSTER.

> Mother, take me to the fields
> in the earliest light of morn,
> there to see the flowers bloom
> when the branches start to sway.

The piano plays a last scale and stops.

AUNT. How precious!

MOTHER. They also know the language of the fan, the language of the gloves, the language of the stamps and the language of the hours. I get goose-flesh when they say that about:

> Twelve o'clock tolls o'er the world
> With horrible sounding rigor;
> Now of the hour of your death
> Bethink yourself, poor sinner.

FIRST AYOLA, *with her mouth full of candy*. Why, what an ugly thing!

MOTHER. And when they say:

> At one we are born
> La ra la, la

And this birth
la, la, ran,
is like opening one's eyes,
lan,
in a bower,
bower, bower.

SECOND AYOLA, *to the sister.* I think the old lady likes to bend the elbow.

To the Mother.

Would you care for another glass?

MOTHER. With consummate pleasure and finest will, as they used to say in my time.

Rosita has been watching for the arrival of the postman.

HOUSEKEEPER. The postman.

General excitement.

AUNT. And he's come just in time.

THIRD SPINSTER. He had to pick his days to arrive on this one.

MOTHER. How fitting!

SECOND AYOLA. Open the letter!

FIRST AYOLA. It's more discreet for you to read it alone. Because at best, he may say something daring.

MOTHER. Heavens!

Rosita leaves with the letter.

FIRST AYOLA. A letter from a sweetheart is not a prayer book.

THIRD SPINSTER. It is a prayer book of love.

SECOND AYOLA. Oh, how refined!

The Ayolas laugh.

FIRST AYOLA. You can tell she never received one.

MOTHER, *strongly.* Fortunately for her!

FIRST AYOLA. That's her problem!

AUNT, *to the Housekeeper, who starts to go out to Rosita.* Where are you going?

HOUSEKEEPER. Can't one take a step around here?

AUNT. Leave her alone!

ROSITA, *entering*. Aunt! Aunt!

AUNT. What's the matter, child?

ROSITA, *excitedly*. Oh, Aunt!

FIRST AYOLA. What?

THIRD SPINSTER. Tell us!

SECOND AYOLA. What?

HOUSEKEEPER. Speak!

AUNT. Out with it!

MOTHER. A glass of water!

SECOND AYOLA. Come.

FIRST AYOLA. Quickly.

Excitement.

ROSITA, *in a choking voice*. Oh, he's getting married!

They all look frightened.

He can't wait any longer, and he wants to marry me, but . . .

SECOND AYOLA, *embracing her*. Hooray! What happiness!

FIRST AYOLA. Give me a hug.

AUNT. Let her speak.

ROSITA, *calmer*. But since he's not able to come right now the marriage will be by proxy and he'll come when he can.

FIRST SPINSTER. Congratulations!

MOTHER, *almost weeping*. May God make you as happy as you deserve to be.

Embraces her.

HOUSEKEEPER. Well, and this proxy? What is it?

ROSITA. Nothing. Just that another person represents the groom in the ceremony.

HOUSEKEEPER. And what else?

ROSITA. Just that one is married then.

HOUSEKEEPER. And at night what?

ROSITA. Heavens!

FIRST AYOLA. Very well said—and at night what?

AUNT. Children!

HOUSEKEEPER. Let him come in person and get married. Proxy! I never heard of it. The bed and its paintings trembling with cold and the bridal clothes in the darkest part of the trunk. Madam, don't you let those proxies come in this house.

They all laugh.

Madam, I don't want any proxies.

ROSITA. But he will come soon. This is just one more proof of how much he loves me.

HOUSEKEEPER. That's it. Let him come—and let him take you by the arm and stir the sugar in your coffee and taste it first to see if it burns.

Laughter. The Uncle comes in bearing a rose.

ROSITA. Uncle!

UNCLE. I have heard everything and almost without knowing what I was doing I cut the only Rosa Mutabile that I had in my greenhouse. It was still red,

> At noon, full-blown,
> She is coral red.

ROSITA.

> Even the sun at the window
> looks in to see her glow.

UNCLE. If I had waited two hours longer to cut it, I would have given it to you white.

ROSITA.

> White like the dove,
> like the laughter of the sea;
> white with the cold whiteness
> of a cheek of salt.

UNCLE. But still, still it has the fire of its youth.

AUNT. Have a little drink with me, husband. This is the day for that.

Excitement. The Third Spinster goes to the piano and plays a polka. Rosita is looking at the rose. The First and Second Spinsters dance with the Ayolas and sing.

> Because I caught a glimpse
> Of you beside the sea,
> Your languor sweet perceived
> Was reason for my sighs;
> And that most subtle sweetness
> Which was my fatal dream,
> Within this moonlight pale,
> In shipwreck here you saw.

The Aunt and Uncle dance. Rosita goes to the pair formed by the Second Spinster and the Ayola. She dances with the Spinster. On seeing the old couple dancing, the Ayola claps her hands; the Housekeeper, upon entering, does likewise.

CURTAIN

ACT THREE

A small living room with green shutters opening on the garden. The stage is silent. A clock strikes six in the evening. The Housekeeper crosses the stage with a box and a suitcase. Ten years have passed. The Aunt appears and sits on a low chair in the center of the stage. Silence. The clock strikes six again. Pause.

HOUSEKEEPER, *entering.* It struck six o'clock twice.

AUNT. And the child?

HOUSEKEEPER. Up there in the tower. And you, where were you?

AUNT. I was taking the last flower pots from the greenhouse.

HOUSEKEEPER. I didn't see you the whole morning.

AUNT. Since my husband died the house is so empty that it seems twice as large, and we even have to search to find each other. Some nights, when I cough in my room I hear an echo as if I were in a church.

HOUSEKEEPER. It's true that the house is now far too large.

AUNT. And then . . . if he were still alive, with that insight he had, with that talent . . .

Almost weeping.

HOUSEKEEPER, *singing.* Lan-lan-van-lan-lan. . . . No, madam. I do not permit crying. He died six years ago and I don't want you to be like the first day. We have cried enough for him! Let us step firmly, madam! Let the sun come around the corners! May he still wait for us many years cutting roses.

AUNT, *rising.* I'm very old, Ama. There is a great ruin weighing down on us.

HOUSEKEEPER. We won't lack for anything. I'm old too!

AUNT. Would that I had your years!

HOUSEKEEPER. There is not much difference between us. But since I have worked a lot I am spry, while your legs have stiffened from so much idleness.

AUNT. You mean to say you think I haven't worked?

HOUSEKEEPER. Just with the tips of your fingers. With threads, with sprouts, with sweetmeats; I, however, have worked with my back, with my knees, with my nails.

AUNT. Then, running a house is not work?

HOUSEKEEPER. It is much more difficult to scrub its floors.

AUNT. I don't want to argue.

HOUSEKEEPER. Well, why not? It will make the time pass. Go ahead. Answer me. But we've grown mute. Before, we used to shout—How about this? How about that? How about the custards? Aren't you going to iron any more? . . .

AUNT. I have resigned myself. . . . One day soup, another day crumbs. My little glass of water and my rosary in my purse; I could wait for death with dignity . . . but when I think of Rosita.

HOUSEKEEPER. That's the wound.

AUNT, *aroused.* When I think of the wrong done her and of the terrible deceit kept up and of the falsity in the heart of that man, who was not of my family nor deserves to be of my family, I would like to be twenty years old to take a boat to Tucumán, snatch up a lash and . . .

HOUSEKEEPER, *interrupting her.* And take a sword and cut off his head and crush it with two stones and cut off that hand with its false vows and lying letters of affection.

AUNT. Yes, yes! To make him pay with blood what has cost blood, even though it should all be my blood. And afterward . . .

HOUSEKEEPER. . . . To scatter the ashes over the sea.

AUNT. To revive him and bring him to Rosita so that I can draw a breath with my honor satisfied.

HOUSEKEEPER. Now, you will admit I was right.

AUNT. I admit it.

HOUSEKEEPER. Over there he found the rich woman he was looking for and married her, but he ought to have told us in time. Because who wants this woman now? She's faded. Madam, couldn't we send him a poisoned letter? So that he would die the instant he opened it?

AUNT. What nonsense! Eight years married and until last month the villain didn't write me the truth. I noticed something in the letters; the power of attorney that didn't come, an air of doubtfulness. . . . He didn't dare . . . but finally he did it. Naturally, after his father had died! And this poor creature, Rosita . . .

HOUSEKEEPER. Shh . . .

AUNT. And remove the two urns.

Rosita appears. She wears a dress of light rose color in the style of 1910. She wears long curls. She has aged much.

HOUSEKEEPER. Child!

ROSITA. What are you doing?

HOUSEKEEPER. Criticizing a little bit. And you, where are you going?

ROSITA. I'm going to the greenhouse. Have they taken the plants already?

AUNT. A few are left.

Rosita leaves. The two women wipe away their tears.

HOUSEKEEPER. And that's all? You sit down and I sit down? And do we just wait to die? And is there no law? And has no one the courage to pulverize him?

AUNT. Hush. Don't go on!

HOUSEKEEPER. I don't have the patience to stand these things without my heart running through my breast as if it were a dog being chased. When I buried my husband, I was very sorry, but at bottom I felt a great joy . . . no, not joy, but my heart quickened to see that I was not the one who was buried. When I buried my little daughter—

do you understand me?—when I buried my little girl it was as if they'd trampled on my insides—but the dead are dead. They're dead—so let's go cry. The door closes, and we keep on living! But this about my Rosita is the worst. It's to love someone and not be able to find him; it's to cry and not to know for whom one weeps; it's to sigh for someone that one knows doesn't deserve those sighs. It is an open wound that gives off without ceasing a little thread of blood and there is no one, no one in the whole world, to bring the cotton wool, the bandages, or the precious piece of ice.

AUNT. What do you want me to do?

HOUSEKEEPER. Let the river carry us along.

AUNT. Everything turns its back on old age.

HOUSEKEEPER. While I have arms you won't lack for anything.

AUNT, *pause. Very low as though with shame.* Ama, I'm not able to pay you any more. You will have to leave us.

HOUSEKEEPER. Wheee! What a blast comes in through the windows! Wheee! Or maybe I'm growing deaf? Well . . . Why do I feel like singing? Just like children coming out of school!

Children's voices are heard.

Do you hear that, madam? My mistress, more my mistress than ever.

Embraces her.

AUNT. Listen!

HOUSEKEEPER. I'm going to make a casserole of mackerel flavored with fennel.

AUNT. Listen!

HOUSEKEEPER. And a snow mountain! I'm going to make you a snow custard covered with colored sugar . . .

AUNT. But, woman! . . .

HOUSEKEEPER, *loudly.* I say! Why, here's Don Martín! Don Martín, come in! Come! Entertain my mistress a little while.

She leaves quickly. Don Martín enters. He is an old man with red hair. He carries a crutch with which he supports a withered leg. A noble type of great dignity with a definite air of sadness.

AUNT. Happy the eyes that see you!

DON MARTÍN. When is the definite moving day?

AUNT. Today.

DON MARTÍN. So you're really going!

AUNT. The new house isn't this one. But it has good views and a little patio with two fig trees where we may have flowers.

DON MARTÍN. It's better like that.

They sit down.

AUNT. And you?

DON MARTÍN. Same old life. I've just come from lecturing to my class in Rhetoric. A real Hell! It was a wonderful lecture: "Concept and Definition of Harmony." But the children weren't interested at all—and what children! For me, since they see I am disabled, they have a little respect. Now and then some pin or other in the chair, or a little paper doll on my back; but to my companions they do horrible things. They are the children of the rich and, since they pay, we can't punish them. This the Director is always telling us. Yesterday they insisted that poor Mr. Canito, the new geography teacher, wore a corset, because his figure is a little bit drawn in; and when he was alone in the patio the big bullies and the boarders undressed him from the waist up, tied him to one of the columns of the corridor and threw a jar of water on him from the balcony.

AUNT. Poor creature!

DON MARTÍN. Every day I enter the school trembling, waiting to see what they are going to do to me. Although, as I say, they respect my misfortune somewhat. A while ago they made a great uproar because Mr. Consuegra, who explains Latin admirably, had found a cat excrement on his class roll.

AUNT. They are devils!

DON MARTÍN. They are the ones who pay and we have to live with them. And, believe me, their parents laugh afterward at their infamies because—since we are assistant teachers and do not give examinations to their sons—they consider us men without feeling—like persons on the lowest level of the class that still wear a tie and an ironed collar.

AUNT. Oh, Don Martín! What a world this is!

DON MARTÍN. What a world! I dreamt always of being a poet. I was born with a talent, a natural flower, and I wrote a play that was never produced.

AUNT. *Jephtha's Daughter?*

DON MARTÍN. That's it.

AUNT. Rosita and I read it. You lent it to us. We read it four or five times.

DON MARTÍN, *eagerly.* And what . . .?

AUNT. I liked it very much. I've always told you that. Especially when she is going to die and she remembers her mother and calls her.

DON MARTÍN. It is strong, isn't it? A real drama. A drama of contour and concept. It was never possible to produce it.

Beginning to recite.

> O mother unexcelled! Now turn your gaze
> to her who lies in abject trance undone;
> receive you these refulgent jewels of mine
> and the horrid death rattle of my combat!

And is this bad? And doesn't this verse sound well as to accent and cesura? "And the horrid death rattle of my combat!"

AUNT. Charming! Charming!

DON MARTÍN. And when Glucinius goes to challenge Isaias and raises the tent's tapestry . . .

HOUSEKEEPER, *interrupting him.* Through here.

Two Workmen dressed in denim suits enter.

FIRST WORKMAN. Good afternoon.

DON MARTÍN'AND AUNT, *together*. Good afternoon.

HOUSEKEEPER. This is it!

She points to a large divan at the back of the room. The men pick it up slowly as if they were carrying a coffin. The Housekeeper follows them. Silence. Two strokes of a bell are heard while the two men cross out with the divan.

DON MARTÍN. Is it the novena of St. Gertrude the Great?

AUNT. Yes, at St. Anthony's.

DON MARTÍN. It's very difficult to be a poet.

The Men go out.

Afterward, I wanted to be a pharmacist. It's a peaceful life.

AUNT. My brother, God rest his soul, was a pharmacist.

DON MARTÍN. But I couldn't. I had to help my mother and I became a teacher. That's why I envied your husband so much. He was what he wanted to be.

AUNT. And it brought him to ruin.

DON MARTÍN. Yes, but my situation is worse.

AUNT. But you go on writing.

DON MARTÍN. I don't know why I write since I have no more hope. But, it's the only thing I like. Did you read my story yesterday? In the second issue of *The Intellectual Granada*?

AUNT. "The Birthday of Matilda"? Yes, we read it. A charming thing.

DON MARTÍN. Yes, isn't it? There I tried to renew myself by writing something with a present-day atmosphere. I even mention an airplane. The truth is, that one has to be modern. But naturally, what I like best are my sonnets.

AUNT. To the nine muses of Parnassus!

DON MARTÍN. To the ten, to the ten! Don't you remember that I named Rosita the tenth muse?

HOUSEKEEPER, *entering*. Mistress, you help me fold this sheet.

The two of them begin folding it.

Don Martín with his little red head! Why didn't you marry, man of God? You wouldn't be so alone in this life!

DON MARTÍN. No one ever loved me!

HOUSEKEEPER. It's just that there's no more taste. With such a precious manner of speaking as you have!

AUNT. Watch out you don't make him fall in love with you!

DON MARTÍN. Let her try!

HOUSEKEEPER. When he lectures in the lower room of the school I go to the coal bin to listen to him: "What is idea?" "The intellectual representation of a thing or an object." Isn't that it?

DON MARTÍN. Look at her! Look at her!

HOUSEKEEPER. Yesterday he was shouting: "No; this is a case of hyperbaton," and then . . . "the epinicion." . . . I'd like to be able to understand, but since I don't understand, it makes me laugh. And the coal man who is always reading a book called *The Ruins of Palmyra* throws glances at me like two fighting-mad cats, but even though I laugh, ignorant as I am, I realize that Don Martín has much merit.

DON MARTÍN. Today no merit is assigned to rhetoric and poetry, nor to a university education.

The Housekeeper goes out quickly with the folded sheet.

AUNT. What can we do! We have very little time left on this stage.

DON MARTÍN. And we must devote that to kindness and sacrifice.

Shouts are heard.

AUNT. What's happening?

HOUSEKEEPER, *appearing*. Don Martín, they want you to go to the school because the children have punctured the water pipes with a nail and all the classrooms are flooded.

DON MARTÍN. Let's go then. I dreamt of Parnassus and I have to be a mason and a plumber. Just so they don't push me or I slip . . .

The Housekeeper helps Don Martín to rise.

HOUSEKEEPER. He's coming! Calm down! Let's hope that the water rises until not a single child is left alive!

DON MARTÍN, *leaving.* God's will be done!

AUNT. Poor thing. What a fate!

HOUSEKEEPER. Let him be a mirror to you! He irons his own collars and darns his own socks. And the time he was sick, when I took him some custard, his bed had some sheets on it that were black as coal, and his walls and his washbasin . . . Oh my!

AUNT. And others have so much.

HOUSEKEEPER. That's why I'll always say: "Damned, damned be the rich!" May not even their fingernails be left!

AUNT. Let them be!

HOUSEKEEPER. But I'm sure that they are going to Hell head-first. Where do you think Don Rafael Salé, exploiter of the poor, who was buried yesterday, can be, God preserve him!—with so many priests and nuns and so much mumbo-jumbo? In Hell! And he will say: "I have twenty million pesetas, don't pinch me with the tongs! I will give you forty thousand duros if you take these coals from my feet!" But the devils, prodding here, prodding there, kicking him for all they're worth, hitting him in the face, until his blood is turned to charcoal . . .

AUNT. All we Christians know that no rich man is going to enter the Kingdom of Heaven, but be careful that you too don't land head-first in Hell for speaking that way.

HOUSEKEEPER. Me, in Hell? The first push I give the furnace of Old Nick will make the hot water reach to the edges of the earth. No, madam, no. I'll get into Heaven by force.

Sweetly.

With you. Each one in an armchair of celestial blue silk, rocking herself, and with fans of scarlet satin. Between the two of us, on a swing of jasmin and rosemary sprigs, Rosita swinging herself, and behind her your husband covered with roses, the way he left this house in his coffin; with the same smile, with the same forehead white as crystal. And you rock like this, and I like this, and Rosita like this, and behind us God throwing roses at us as if the three of us were a mother-of-pearl float in a Holy Week procession full of wax candles and flounces.

AUNT. And let the handkerchiefs for tears stay here below.

HOUSEKEEPER. That's it! Confusion to them! For us, a celestial blow out!

AUNT. Because we don't have a single tear left within our hearts!

FIRST WORKMAN, *entering.* At your service.

HOUSEKEEPER. Come!

As they are leaving, from the door.

Courage!

AUNT. God bless you!

The Aunt sits down slowly. Rosita appears with a package of letters in her hand. Silence.

Have they taken the bureau?

ROSITA. Just now. Your cousin Esperanza sent a child for a screwdriver.

AUNT. They are probably putting together the beds for tonight. We should have gone early and done things as we wanted them. My cousin has probably placed the furniture just anywhere.

ROSITA. But I'd rather leave here when the street is dark. If I could I'd put out the street lamp. The neighbors will be watching for us anyway. With the moving the door has been full of children all day as if there were a dead person in the house.

AUNT. If I had known, I would by no means have permitted your uncle to mortgage the house with furniture and everything. What we have left are the barest necessities. A chair to sit on and a bed to sleep in.

ROSITA. To die in.

AUNT. That was a fine thing he did for us! Tomorrow the new owners come. I would like your uncle to see us. Foolish old man! Weak in business matters. Addled with his roses! A man with no idea of the value of money! He bankrupted me day by day. "Mr. So-and-So is here." And he would say: "Show him in." And he would come in with empty pockets and leave with them overflowing with silver. And always: "Don't let my wife find out." The extravagant thing! The weakling! And there was no calamity he didn't remedy, nor children he did not take in because . . . because . . . he had the greatest heart a man ever had . . . the purest Christian soul. . . . No, no. Be quiet, old lady! Be quiet, babbler, and respect God's will! Penniless! Very well. So, silence! But I see you . . .

ROSITA. Don't worry about me, Aunt. I know that the mortgage was to pay for my furniture and my trousseau, and that's what hurts me.

AUNT. He did right. You deserved everything and everything he bought is worthy of you and will be beautiful the day you use it.

ROSITA. The day I use it?

AUNT. Of course, your wedding day.

ROSITA. Don't make me speak of it.

AUNT. That's a failing of the "decent" women of these parts. Not speaking! We don't speak, but we have to speak.

Shouting.

Ama! Has the postman come?

ROSITA. What do you propose to do?

AUNT. Live—and let you take a lesson from me.

ROSITA, *embracing her.* Hush!

AUNT. I have to speak out sometime. Leave your four walls, my child. Don't give yourself over to misfortune.

ROSITA, *kneeling before her.* I've grown accustomed to living for many years outside of myself, thinking of things

that were far away, and now that these things no longer
exist, I continue going around and around in a cold place,
looking for a way out that I shall never find. I knew everything. I knew he had married; some kind soul took care to
tell me that. And I have been believing his letters with a
sobbing illusion that surprised even me. If people had not
talked; if you had not learned it; if no one but I had known
of it; his letters and his lie would have fed my illusion like
the first year of his absence. But every one knew it, and
I found myself pointed out with a finger that made my
engaged girl's modesty ridiculous, and gave a grotesque air
to my maidenly fan. Every year that passed was like an
intimate garment torn from my body. And today one friend
gets married, and another and another, and tomorrow she
has a son and he grows up and comes to show me his
examination marks, and they build new houses and make
new songs and I stay the same, with the same trembling,
the same; I, just as before, cutting the same carnations,
looking at the same clouds; and one day out walking I
realize I don't know anybody. Girls and boys leave me
behind because I get tired, and one of them says, "There's
the old maid," and another, beautiful, with a curly head,
comments: "No one would cast an eye at her any more."
And I hear it, and I can't even cry out, but go on, with a
mouth full of poison and an overpowering desire to flee,
to take off my shoes, to rest, and never, never move out of
my corner again.

AUNT. Child! Rosita!

ROSITA. I'm old. Yesterday I heard the housekeeper say
that I could still marry. By no means! Don't think it. I lost
all hope of marrying the one I loved with all my blood, the
one I loved and still do. Everything is finished, and yet,
with all illusion lost, I go to bed and get up again with the
most terrible of all feelings—the feeling of having hope
dead. I want to flee. I don't want to see. I want to be left
serene, empty. Doesn't a poor woman have the right to
breathe freely? And yet, hope pursues me, encircles me,
bites me; like a dying wolf tightening his grip for the last
time.

AUNT. Why didn't you listen to me? Why didn't you marry another?

ROSITA. I was tied. And besides, what man came to this house sincerely to gain my affection overflowing with tenderness? Not one.

AUNT. You wouldn't pay attention to any of them. You were blinded by a deceiver.

ROSITA. I've always been serious.

AUNT. You clung to your idea without regard to reality and without thinking of your future.

ROSITA. I am as I am. And I can't make myself change. Now the only thing left for me is my dignity. What is inside of me, I keep to myself.

AUNT. That's what I don't want.

HOUSEKEEPER, *coming in suddenly.* Nor I either! Speak, unburden yourself, we'll cry until the three of us are tired and we will share our feelings.

ROSITA. And what am I going to tell you? There are things that cannot be told because there are no words to tell them; and even if there were, no one would understand their meaning. You understand me if I ask for bread or water, or even for a kiss, but you would never be able to understand, nor remove, this dark hand that freezes or burns my heart—I don't know which—every time I'm left alone.

HOUSEKEEPER. You're saying something now.

AUNT. There's consolation for everything.

ROSITA. It would be a never-ending story. I know that my eyes will always be young, but I also know that my back will bend more each day. After all, what has happened to me has happened to a thousand women.

Pause.

But why am I saying all this?

To the Housekeeper.

You go straighten things up, because in a few minutes we're going to leave this house with its garden; and you, Aunt, please don't worry about me.

Pause. To the Housekeeper.

Go on! I don't like you to look at me like that. Those glances of a faithful dog bother me.

The Housekeeper leaves.

Those pitying looks that perturb and anger me.

AUNT. Child, what do you want me to do?

ROSITA. Leave me as a lost thing.

Pause. She walks up and down.

I know you are remembering your sister, the old maid . . . the old maid like me. She was bitter and hated children and every one who put on a new dress . . . but I won't be like that.

Pause.

I ask your forgiveness.

AUNT. What nonsense.

At the back, an eighteen-year-old Youth appears.

ROSITA. Come in.

YOUTH. But . . . are you moving?

ROSITA. In a few minutes. When it grows dark.

AUNT. Who is it?

ROSITA. It's María's son.

AUNT. Which María?

ROSITA. The oldest of the three Manolas.

AUNT. Oh, those
                Who go up to the Alhambra,
                by threes and fours, alone.

Forgive my bad memory, son.

YOUTH. You've seen me very few times.

AUNT. Yes, but I was very fond of your mother. How charming she was! She died about the same time as my husband.

ROSITA. Before.

YOUTH. Eight years ago.

ROSITA. He has her face.

YOUTH, *happy*. Not quite. Mine was made with a hammer.

AUNT. And the same spirit; the same character!

YOUTH. Why, of course I resemble her. At carnival time I put on one of mother's dresses . . . a dress she had a long time ago, green . . .

ROSITA, *melancholy*. With black laces . . . and Nile-green silk flounces.

YOUTH. Yes.

ROSITA. And a great bow of velvet at the waist.

YOUTH. The same.

ROSITA. Falling on either side of the bustle.

YOUTH. Exactly. What an absurd style!

He smiles.

ROSITA, *sad*. It was a pretty style!

YOUTH. Don't tell me that! Well, I was coming down the stairs almost dying of laughter with that old thing on, filling all the corridor with the smell of mothballs, and suddenly my aunt began to cry bitterly because she said it was exactly like seeing my mother. It made an impression on me, naturally, and I left the dress and the mask on my bed.

ROSITA. There is nothing more alive than a memory. It comes to the point of making our lives impossible. That's why I well understand those drunken little old women who go through the streets trying to blot out the world, and sit singing on the benches of the promenade.

AUNT. And your aunt, the married one?

YOUTH. She writes from Barcelona. Each time less.

ROSITA. Had she any children?

YOUTH. Four of them.

Pause.

HOUSEKEEPER, *entering*. Give me the keys to the wardrobe.

The Aunt gives them to her. Then, referring to the Youth.

Here, this young man was walking yesterday with his sweetheart. I saw them at the new plaza. She wanted to go one way and he wouldn't let her.

Laughs.

AUNT. Come now, leave the boy alone!

YOUTH, *confused.* We were just joking.

HOUSEKEEPER, *leaving.* Don't blush!

ROSITA. Now be quiet.

The Housekeeper leaves.

YOUTH. What a beautiful garden you have!

ROSITA. We used to have!

AUNT. Come and cut some flowers.

YOUTH. I hope everything goes well with you, Doña Rosita.

ROSITA. God go with you, child!

Aunt and Youth leave. Evening is falling.

Doña Rosita! Doña Rosita!

> She opens in the morning
> red as blood.
> The evening turns her white
> with a whiteness of spume and salt
> and when the night arrives
> her petals begin to rain.

Pause.

HOUSEKEEPER, *comes in with a shawl.* Let us be going.

ROSITA. Yes. I am going to throw on a coat.

HOUSEKEEPER. Since I have taken down the clothes rack, you will find it hanging on the window handle.

The Third Spinster comes in wearing a dark dress with a mourning veil on her head and a ribbon round her neck as worn in 1912. They speak low.

THIRD SPINSTER. Ama!

HOUSEKEEPER. You find us here for only a few more minutes.

THIRD SPINSTER. I came to give a piano lesson nearby and dropped in to see if you needed something.

HOUSEKEEPER. May God repay you!

THIRD SPINSTER. What a catastrophe!

HOUSEKEEPER. Yes, yes. But don't touch my heart. Don't lift this veil of sorrow because I am the one who has to give encouragement in this wake without a corpse that you are witnessing.

THIRD SPINSTER. I'd like to see them.

HOUSEKEEPER. But it's better for you not to see them. Go to the other house.

THIRD SPINSTER. That's better. But if you need something, you know that I'm here to do anything I can.

HOUSEKEEPER. This misfortune will surely pass!

The wind is heard.

THIRD SPINSTER. A wind has come up.

HOUSEKEEPER. Yes, it looks like rain.

The Third Spinster leaves.

AUNT, *entering.* If this wind keeps up there won't be a rose left alive. The cypresses near the arbor almost touch the wall of my room. It's almost as if someone wanted to make the garden ugly so that we should feel no pain at leaving it.

HOUSEKEEPER. If you are talking about beauty, beautiful it has never been. Have you put on your coat? And this scarf. That's it. Well covered.

Puts it around her.

Now when we get there, dinner will be ready. For dessert, custard. You like it. A custard as golden as a marigold.

The Housekeeper speaks with a voice choked by deep emotion. A thud is heard.

AUNT. That's the greenhouse door. Why don't you close it?

HOUSEKEEPER. It can't be closed because of the dampness.

AUNT. It will be banging all night.

HOUSEKEEPER. Well, since we won't hear it . . . !

The stage is in the sweet half-light of evening.

AUNT. I will. I'll hear it.

Rosita appears. She is pale, dressed in white, with a coat down to the hem of her dress.

HOUSEKEEPER, *courageously.* Let's go!

ROSITA, *in a weak voice.* It's begun to rain. Like this there will be no one at the balconies to see us leave.

AUNT. That's preferable.

ROSITA, *wavers a little, leans against a chair, and falls, supported by the Housekeeper and the Aunt, who prevent her from fainting completely.*
> And when the night arrives
> her petals begin to rain.

They leave and at their exit the stage is left empty. The door is heard banging. Suddenly a French door at the back opens and the white curtains flutter in the wind.

CURTAIN

THE BUTTERFLY'S EVIL SPELL

A COMEDY IN TWO ACTS
AND A PROLOGUE

(1919)

CHARACTERS

DOÑA BEETLE

WITCHBEETLE

SYLVIA BEETLE

DOÑA PROUDBEETLE, MOTHER OF SYLVIA

BUTTERFLY

BOYBEETLE, SON OF DOÑA BEETLE

SCORPY, THE WOODCUTTER

FIRST FIREFLY

SECOND FIREFLY

THIRD FIREFLY

SAINTBEETLE

FIRST FIELDBEETLE

SECOND FIELDBEETLE

OTHER FIELDBEETLES

GUARDBEETLES

TWO GIRLBEETLES

PROLOGUE

Ladies and Gentlemen: The play you're about to hear is of no great consequence, and yet, disturbing. A kind of defeated comedy about someone who, reaching for the moon, reached only his own heartbreak. Love, that love which with its ironies and misfortunes occurs in the world of men, here occurs in a deep meadow populated only by insects—a meadow where life, but that was a long time ago, was serene and undisturbed. These insects led lives of contentment. They had nothing to worry about except peacefully drinking their dewdrops and bringing up their children in the saintly fear of their gods. They made love to each other out of habit, without worrying about it. For love was given from father to son like a jewel old and exquisite, a jewel which had been passed to the first insect by the hand of God. With the same calm and certainty with which a blossom surrenders its pollen to the wind, they enjoyed making love to each other under the lush green grasses.

Ah, but one day there was an insect who attempted to go beyond this love. He formed an attachment for something quite far away from his mode of living. Perhaps he had read, with great difficulty, some book left on the grass by one of the few poets who visit the country, and had been contaminated by one of those poems that start out, "O, Woman Unattainable, you I love." That's why I beg all of you never to strew books of poems about the countryside; you might cause great desolation among the insects. The sort of poetry that questions why stars move in their orbits is very harmful to little souls not yet completely formed. Needless to say, the lovelorn little creature died. Because Death disguises itself as Love. How many times that huge skeleton carrying a scythe—which we see portrayed in prayer books—takes the form of a woman in

order to deceive us and to open the door into darkness.
Cupid himself, it almost seems, sleeps in the skull's
hollow round chambers. In how many ancient tales does a
flower, a kiss or a glance do the terrible office of a dagger.

An old wood sylph, escaped from one of the great
Shakespeare's books—a sylph who now wanders through
the meadows propping up his dried-out wings with a pair
of crutches—told the writer this story one autumn at night-
fall, when the flocks were safe in the fold; and now the
writer tells it to you, cloaked in its own melancholy. But
before beginning, I want to make the same plea to you
that the old wood sylph made to the writer that autumn
evening when the flocks were in the fold. "Why do the
clean, bright insects, moving so charmingly through the
grass, cause a feeling of repugnance in you? And why is it
that you men, full of sins and incurable vices, are filled
with loathing for the good grubs who creep quietly along
in the meadows, taking the sun of a warm morning? What
right do you have to scorn the meanest of God's creatures?
Until you learn to love deeply the stones and the cater-
pillars, you will not enter the Kingdom of Heaven." And
the old sylph said this to the writer also: "The kingdom of
plants and animals is near at hand; though Man forgets
his Maker, plants and animals are very near the light.
And, Poet, tell men that love is born with the same exalta-
tion in all planes of life—that the rhythm of a leaf swaying
in the wind is the same as that of a distant star, and that
the very words spoken by the fountain in the shade are
repeated by the sea, and in the same tone. Tell Man to be
humble. In nature, all things are equal." The old sylph was
silent then. Now, listen to the play. Perhaps you'll only
smile to hear these insects talk like men or like youngsters.
But if you draw some deep lesson from it, go out to the
wood and speak a word of thanks to the sylph with the
crutches, some tranquil evening when the flocks are in
the fold.

ACT ONE

*The stage represents a lowly green meadow in the dense
shade of a great cypress. A little path, almost invisible,
embroiders an innocent arabesque over the grass. Beyond
the meadow there is a small pond bordered by splendid
lilies and blue stones. It is the clean hour of dawn and
all the meadow is covered with dew. The burrows of
the insects, like a tiny and fantastic town of caves, can
be seen bordering on the paths. Doña Beetle comes out
of her house carrying a little handful of grass that serves
her as a broom. She is a very old beetle with one leg
missing—lost in consequence of a blow from a broom
received in a house where she was lodging while she
was still young and shining. The dawn's great hammers
redden the horizon's cold sheet.*

SCENE 1

DOÑA BEETLE AND WITCHBEETLE

DOÑA BEETLE, *looking out over the meadow.*
>   Oh, what a clear and serene morning!
>   Day's first light is shining.

WITCHBEETLE, *wearing a cone-shaped hat embroidered
with stars and a robe of dry moss.*
>   Good neighbor mine, God's blessings on you.

DOÑA BEETLE.
>   Where are you going, so full of dew?

WITCHBEETLE.
>   I come from dreams of being a flower
>   lying hidden in the grass.

DOÑA BEETLE.
> How did you dream this?

WITCHBEETLE.
> In my dream, the drops of dew
> are loving lips that blow me kisses
> and sprinkle with stars my somber robe.

DOÑA BEETLE, *grumbling*.
> Just don't forget that writing poetry . . .

WITCHBEETLE, *sadly*.
> Oh, Doña Beetle, what's on your mind?

DOÑA BEETLE.
> . . . is a fine way to catch a pneumonia
> that'll put an end to all your brains.
> We'd all of us, of course, regret that very much.

WITCHBEETLE.
> My heart with sorrow is laden, neighbor!
> Yesterday afternoon a swallow told me
> that the light of the stars is growing dim.
> God has fallen asleep; and in the wood
> I saw a star, all red and trembling,
> dropping its petals like a rose.
> I saw it perish
> and then felt fall
> inside my heart
> something like nighttime.
> "Crickets, my friends!" I cried. "Do you see the
>   stars?"
> "A fairy has died." That's what they answered me.
> I went close to the trunk of the old oak tree
> and saw there, dead, the fairy of field and sea.

DOÑA BEETLE.
> Who could have killed her?

WITCHBEETLE.
> She was killed by love.

DOÑA BEETLE.
> Look up where the dawn is breaking.

WITCHBEETLE.
And your good son, how is he?

DONA BEETLE.
Fine.

WITCHBEETLE.
Yesterday I thought he looked sad.

DOÑA BEETLE.
I noticed that too.
He's fallen in love.

WITCHBEETLE.
With Sylvia, perhaps?

DOÑA BEETLE.
He's says it's with something he'll never possess.

WITCHBEETLE.
He's going to be a poet, and no wonder,
since his father was one.

DOÑA BEETLE.
A great disappointment
I had in that one.

WITCHBEETLE.
He was a charmer.

DOÑA BEETLE.
He was a wife beater.

WITCHBEETLE.
But he always kept the trough full.

DOÑA BEETLE.
And it didn't keep him from being a good man.

WITCHBEETLE.
There's no more to be said, I loved him a lot.
Now, what about your crippled leg?

DOÑA BEETLE.
Last night I noticed again
that mean little twinge that bothers me so.

WITCHBEETLE.
Try applying daisy petals.

Bathe it in dew and stay off your feet.
Take this holy, ground ant-skull powder
at night with some round-leaved mint.

DOÑA BEETLE.

Friend,
may the Great Beetle repay you in love
and turn you in your dreams into a flower.

Comforting her.

Throw off sadnes and melancholy.
Life is pleasant; its days are few;
The only time to enjoy it is now.

WITCHBEETLE, *as though dreaming.*
The light of the stars is growing dim.

DOÑA BEETLE.
Don't think of that now, my learned neighbor;
look at the joy this dawn will bring.

WITCHBEETLE.
But oh, what I saw there where the oak trees grow.

DOÑA BEETLE.
Don't think about it; just go off to bed.

WITCHBEETLE, *in a brusque transition back to reality.*
Silent the meadow.
Now the dew rises to its heaven unknown.
The whispering breezes
fragrantly to us are blown.

DOÑA BEETLE.
Oh, are you a poet too, my learned neighbor?
We poor folk with our cooking
have enough to do.

WITCHBEETLE.
Don't you be commonplace.

DOÑA BEETLE, *a little disgusted.*
In my class we all know how to sing
and suck juice from flowers. What do you take us
for?

WITCHBEETLE.

>No wonder your husband hit you.
>Cooking and poetry can be combined.
>Till later, friend; I'm going to rest.

Exits.

DOÑA BEETLE.

>May the light guide you.
>>I'm going to sweep
>my doorstep off with the morning breeze.

She starts to sweep, singing.

>There's a worm that every evening
>to me of his love sings.
>I won't say yes till he's developed
>four little feet and wings.

SCENE 2

DOÑA BEETLE AND SYLVIA

From stage left comes the petite Sylvia Beetle, high-spirited and bright-eyed. In her particular class of repugnant insect, she is enchanting. She gleams like jet and her legs are quick and delicate. She is the daughter of Doña Proudbeetle, is more than a year old and is the best match in town. She is carrying as a parasol a tiny daisy with which she plays charmingly and wears on her head deliciously a ladybug's golden shell.

DOÑA BEETLE.

>You're out very early,
>bewitching and beautiful girl.

SYLVIA.

>You call me girl? I was graduated
>from school some time ago.

DOÑA BEETLE.

> Does it upset you to be called
> a child? Then I'll call you girl,
> or little girl.

SYLVIA, *coquettishly.*

>   No, it's not that.

DOÑA BEETLE.

> Then what's the matter with you?

SYLVIA.

> Sorrows, that I'm always suffering
> without anybody knowing.

DOÑA BEETLE.

> So young and so sad already?
> It's all very well for the old
> witchbeetle to be sad, but you
> are much too new here yet—
> the world is yours for the asking.

SYLVIA, *ingenuously.*

> All I've ever seen of it is this neighborhood.

DOÑA BEETLE, *musingly.*

> Did that witchbeetle tell you
> that the starlight is going out
> because a fairy—or something
> or other—has died?

SYLVIA.

> She's told me nothing.

DOÑA BEETLE.

>   Well, then,
> why all this sadness
> consuming and dragging you down?
> What is your trouble?

SYLVIA.

>   Oh, Granny dear,
> where was your heart
> when you were young? What if I told you
> that all of me is nothing but heart?

DOÑA BEETLE, *in a burst of indignation.*
> You're all of you poets around here.
> And while you're mooning over your poetry,
> your homes and your housework can go hang.
> You're a pack of shameless hussies
> who sleep anywhere but at home
> and heaven knows with whom.

SYLVIA.
>   It's patience
> one needs to listen to you.
> You're insulting.

DOÑA BEETLE.
>   I'm not trying
> to insult you, Sylvia, child;
> it's just very upsetting for me
> to see you so sad and desolate
> when you've no cause to be.

SYLVIA.
>   My sorrows
> do have a cause—one certain cause.

DOÑA BEETLE, *affectionately.*
> Can't I help you with them, child?

SYLVIA.
> My troubles are deep ones,
> deep as that lagoon.

In anguish.
> Where lies the water,
> tranquil and serene,
> where I may still
> my questing thirst?

DOÑA BEETLE, *frightened.*
> Sylvia, please calm yourself.
> Use more judgment and be at peace.

SYLVIA, *throwing the daisy on the floor.*
> On which footpath
> over this meadow

can I go to another world
where I shall find love?

DOÑA BEETLE, *forcefully*.
This is absurd, Sylvia.
You're going crazy.

SYLVIA.
                                                      Much time
is left me to shed my tears.
I shall inter myself 'neath these sands
and hope that some kind lover
will come disinter me with his love.

DOÑA BEETLE.
You're very deep in love,
I can see that. But in my time
we young ladies didn't ask
for sweethearts at the top of our lungs.
Neither did we talk in parables
the way you do. Modesty
went a little further
than in these times. There was a tale
of a very saintly beetle lady
who remained a spinster
and lived six years. But here am I,
just two months old, and old already.
All because I got married. Oh!

Sheds a few tears.

SYLVIA, *very romantically*.
Oh, love, to be able to know you.
You're sweet and black, they say.
Black your tiny wings,
black your form entire,
like night, when no stars shine.
Emeralds your eyes,
violets your legs.

DOÑA BEETLE.
You're crazier than a cricket
I once knew over there in his cave

who gave himself out to be
a great magician and a prophet.
He was a poor wretch
but he gave me a prescription
good for curing lovesickness.

SYLVIA, *intrigued*.
What did the prescription say?

DOÑA BEETLE.
"Give every one in love
two knocks across the pate
and never, never let them
go tumbling in the grass."

SYLVIA.
You're laughing at me, Señora.

DOÑA BEETLE.
Sylvia, who wouldn't laugh,
seeing such a pretty girl
do so many foolish things?

SYLVIA, *aside*.
What she doesn't know is that
it's her son whom I love.

DOÑA BEETLE.
                              Nevertheless,
how discreet of you not to mention
the one who's the cause of your troubles.
And where might your love be—
very far away?

SYLVIA.
                              So very near is he
his breath is on every breeze.

DOÑA BEETLE.
A young man from the village!
You've certainly kept it quiet.
Does he love you?

SYLVIA.
                              He detests me.

DOÑA BEETLE.
> That's odd. You're rich.
> Now, in my time . . .

SYLVIA.
>   The princess
> he's hoping for will never come.

DOÑA BEETLE.
> What is he like?

SYLVIA.
>   I thrill with delight
> at his little body and his eyes
> dreamy as a poet's.
> He has a yellow mole
> on his right leg
> and yellow are the heavenly
> points of his antennae.

DOÑA BEETLE.
> Why, that's my son.

SYLVIA.
> I love him unto madness.

DOÑA BEETLE, *as though dreaming.*
> And she's rich. How stupid
> of this strange child.
> I'll force my son to love her.

Sadly, pretending what she doesn't feel.
> Ah, how you must suffer!

Aside.
> She has a magnificent income.
> Poor little thing, flesh of my flesh
> and blood of my own arteries,
> I'll marry you to my son.

SYLVIA, *blushing with shame.*
> Oh! You've guessed it!

DOÑA BEETLE, *embracing her affectionately.*
>   Remember,
> I wasn't born yesterday—
> I guessed what your sorrow was.

SYLVIA.

Oh, what joy! What happiness!

DOÑA BEETLE, *winning in the extreme*.

There now, clean this darling face
and shake these foolish little tears off
right here beneath the lilies.
I'm going to call my son
so he can see you.

SYLVIA

The queen

I shall be, of this green meadow,
for I have love and wealth.

SCENE 3

BOYBEETLE, DOÑA BEETLE AND SYLVIA

*The Boybeetle is a trim and refined little boy whose dis-
tinction derives from painting the tips of his antennae
and his right leg with lily pollen. He is a poet and a
visionary who, coached by the Witchbeetle, whose pupil
he is, awaits a certain great revelation which is to decide
his life's course. In one of his feet—hands—he carries a bit
of tree bark on which he has been writing a poem. Doña
Beetle walks beside him extolling Sylvia's income. The
latter dedicates herself to flirting, moving the daisy parasol from one side to the other; then, placing her little
paw on her face, sighing enrapturedly. By now the sun
shines brightly.*

BOYBEETLE, *aside*.

No, I don't want to get married, Mother.
I've told you a thousand times
I don't want to get married.

DOÑA BEETLE, *weeping*.

You're just determined to torture me.

BOYBEETLE.

> Mother, I don't love her.

DOÑA BEETLE.

> That doesn't make any difference.

BOYBEETLE.

> Without love I refuse to get married.

DOÑA BEETLE.

> She owns a piece of glass,
> a precious gem found
> by her grandfather one night,
> very blue—he thought
> it was a piece of sky.
> She has a spacious house,
> a well-filled trough—
> look at her!—she's a rose!
> Go flatter her, discreetly.
> Tell her that you love
> her little starlike face—
> that you spend the hours
> thinking only of her.
> You've got to get married.
> Do it now, just for me!

Raising her voice.

> I've some cooking to do.
> I'll leave you two here alone.

Exits.

SCENE 4

SYLVIA AND THE BOYBEETLE

Sylvia wards off the sun with the daisy and sighs longingly. The boy sits on a white pebble and waves his antennae slowly.

BOYBEETLE, *reading from the bark which he carries in his foot-hand.*

O scarlet poppy who o'er all the meadow gaze,
would that I were as lovely as you;
your gown paints the sky with a scarlet haze,
weeping for the daybreak's dew.

You are the star that gives our village its light.
But may my eyes go blind ere I see the sight
of your stem, without light or warmth, turned yel-
     low,
and your leaves withered and your color sallow.

Would that I were an ant, on you I could gaze
without your slender stem breaking.
I'd like to be with you the rest of my days,
with April-honey kisses for our love-making.

In my kisses the warmth and sweetness lie
of the fire whence lives my passion rare,
and from now till the day I die
this heart for you will always care.

SYLVIA, *aside, dream-rapt.*
     What a passionate madrigal
     that was he sang!
Turning to the boy.
     A very good day to you. How are you?
BOYBEETLE.
     Fine, and you?
SYLVIA.

                                   I am . . .
     forever on the search for one thing.
BOYBEETLE.
     What thing?
SYLVIA.

                                   Love.
BOYBEETLE.
     That's very hard to find.
SYLVIA.
     My heart searches for kisses.

BOYBEETLE.

You'll get them.

SYLVIA.

I think not.

When are you ever going to get married?

BOYBEETLE.

Alas, my dream
is lost in that star
which resembles a flower.

SYLVIA.

Might it not easily wilt
in the heat of the sun?

BOYBEETLE.

I have the cooling water
its fever to allay.

SYLVIA.

And where is your star?

BOYBEETLE.

In my imagination.

SYLVIA, *sadly*.

Well, one day you'll see it.

BOYBEETLE.

I'll be its troubadour.
I'll recite it madrigals
to the wind's sweet sound.

SYLVIA.

Do you remember the evening
when, on the flowering path,
you said to me, "I love you?"

BOYBEETLE.

All that is past.
I don't love you now, Sylvia.

SYLVIA, *weeping*.

I know that.

BOYBEETLE.

I beg you,

please don't cry.

SYLVIA.

> My heart aches.
> (Oh, poor me! He doesn't love me.)

BOYBEETLE, *coming near to console her.*

> Oh, Lord, don't cry any more.

Just as they are very close together two unruly little Girl-beetles come down the street. One of them has a fly tied on a blade of dried grass.

GIRLBEETLES, *shrieking.*

> The boy and girl sweethearts!
> Yah, yah, yah!

SYLVIA.

> If it were only true—
> what the children say. . . .

BOYBEETLE.

> Don't cry, little Sylvia.

SYLVIA.

> My heart aches.

GIRLBEETLES, *leaving.*

> The boy and girl sweethearts,
> yah, yah, yah!

SYLVIA.

> Alas, I'm so unfortunate.

BOYBEETLE.

> What a sad state of affairs.

SCENE 5

SCORPY, THE WOODCUTTER, SYLVIA, BOYBEETLE, DOÑA
BEETLE AND, LATER, DOÑA PROUDBEETLE

The Boybeetle quickly moves away from Sylvia when he sees Scorpy, the Woodcutter, coming. Scorpy is an old woodchopper who lives in the forest and comes to the village regularly to get drunk. He is an insatiable glutton

*and a very bad person. He speaks in a brandy-roughened
voice.*

BOYBEETLE.
>   Dry your tears.

SYLVIA.
>   I will.

SCORPY, *coming in drunk, singing and staggering.*
>   For the little leaves of mint
>   are sweet—oh my!—to pluck.
>   Tatará, tarará, tatará,

He scratches his head with his monstrous pincer.
>   Livestock in the headpiece.

Singing.
>   Tatará, tatará, tatará.

To the Boybeetle.
>   Hello, boy.

To Sylvia, as he comically waves his pincer.
>   Oh, Your Highness,
>   Holy Saint Beetle grant you peace.

The other two are very uneasy.
>   Am I in your way, perhaps,
>   in this blooming meadow?
>   Are you talking about love,
>   and planning to build a nest?
>   If I bother you, I'll go away,

*Winking maliciously and giving the Boybeetle a poke in
his stomach with his pincer.*
>   so you can kiss.

BOYBEETLE, *very angry.*
>   You may stay.

SCORPY.
>   I will.

BOYBEETLE.
>   How impertinent.

SCORPY.
>   The enjoyment
>   of love is proper to spring.

You, being a poet,
must know many's the thing.

BOYBEETLE, *indignant*.
Now be quiet.

SCORPY.
Why, I never open my mouth.
I don't even know how to talk!
I was raised at home,
in the middle of an olive grove.

SYLVIA, *very sadly*.
Oh!

SCORPY.
What's the matter, lovely brunette?

SYLVIA.
Nothing.

SCORPY.
Nothing? That's funny!
Got mother-in-law trouble?

SYLVIA.
Idiot!

SCORPY.
The alistogracy
have their troubles too.
That's my philosophy.
For many are the misfortunes
of this long life.
And even though I'm poor, I'm honest.
Supposing I do get drunk. All right;
don't people get drunk?
I'm an innocent old man.

BOYBEETLE, *aside*.
A scoundrel.

SYLVIA.
A glutton.

SCORPY.
Which of us
does not admit to defects?

I'm very fond of eating,
but I'm a very worthy person.

BOYBEETLE.

Shut up and go back to your woods.

SYLVIA.

Leave us alone now, brother.

SCORPY, *undaunted and with great relish.*

Right now I just finished eating a mammaworm.
She was delicious, squashy and toothsome—a treat!—
nursing at her side a tender little boyworm.

Sylvia and the Boybeetle are horrified.

But I wouldn't touch him; he revolted me.

SYLVIA.

Holy Saint Beetle!

BOYBEETLE.

Why would you hurt anyone?

SCORPY, *carried away, not hearing.*

I wouldn't eat it because it was nursing
and because I like them bigger—now you know!

BOYBEETLE.

You criminal!
Don't you know, you villain, you've broken a home,
killing that poor little motherworm for food?

SCORPY.

If you'd like me to, I'll beat my breast,
then let Saint Beetle pardon me.

BOYBEETLE.

Murder
is serious—a sin He won't pardon.

SYLVIA.

Oh, poor little motherless babyworms!

SCORPY, *with irony.*

Oh, you poets!
If you knew what a sweet-tasting skin she had.

BOYBEETLE.

You make me furious!

SYLVIA, *forcefully*.

What a beast!

SCORPY, *with relish*.

Hold your tongues.

Both of you are highly edible.

SYLVIA.

I'm scared.

She runs to take refuge in Doña Beetle's cottage.

BOYBEETLE, *terrified, hides behind the stone on which he was seated.*

Scorpy!

SCORPY.

I can eat your flesh up and be
just the same old me.
But never fear, I'm one who tends
always to respect old friends.

From her little cave Doña Beetle comes out in a fury and limping, followed by Sylvia, terribly frightened and weeping.

DOÑA BEETLE, *shouting*.

You great scoundrel!
You hopeless drunk.
See how you've frightened them.

SCORPY, *grinning like a cat*.

All in jest, Señora.

DOÑA BEETLE, *to the boy*.

Oh, what a state you're in.
My darling! You villain!
Poor Sylvia!

SCORPY, *aside*.

I could eat
her legs with relish.

DOÑA BEETLE.

Villain.

SCORPY.

Because of your gray hairs,
I respect you, Señora.

To the Boybeetle.

> Don't be afraid, my boy.

BOYBEETLE, *distrustfully.*

> Who's afraid?

DOÑA BEETLE, *aside, to Sylvia, and furious.*

>   Impossible.

SYLVIA.

> He doesn't love me, I tell you.
> He told me he is in love
> with a flower.

DOÑA BEETLE.

>   The idiot!

> But I'll fix it so he'll love you.

SCORPY, *drunker by the minute, to the boy.*

> She had a busted leg
> and I ate her.
> She was a lovely spider.

Laughing in great peals.

> She was so flavorsome.

BOYBEETLE, *frightened out of his skin by the prospect of being devoured by this panther in the form of a scorpion, speaks in a trembling voice.*

> How did you manage to trick her
> into being caught?

SCORPY, *leaping on the boy.*

>   Like this!

BOYBEETLE, *screaming.*

> Oh, Mother, he'll kill me!

He gets away from Scorpy and flies to his mother.

DOÑA BEETLE, *up in arms.*

> Go away, you unspeakable villain.

SCORPY, *teetering.*

> Don't be so chicken-hearted!

During this scene, the Girlbeetle who went by earlier with the fly on the leash has reappeared. Scorpy catches sight of her, grabs up her fly and swallows it.

GIRLBEETLE, *weeping and shrieking*.
> Oh, my fly! My fly!

SCORPY.
> Oh, what a delicious treat.

SYLVIA, *throwing her arms around Doña Beetle*.
> Help, oh help! He'll eat us alive!

SCORPY, *in cavernous tones, to frighten them*.
> I shall devour you!

GIRLBEETLE, *flying, terrified*.
> Oh, mamma, I'm afraid!

Offstage the sound of voices and of cries of compassion are heard.

SYLVIA.
> What's that?

DOÑA BEETLE.
> What's happening?

A group of Fieldbeetles enters carrying in their arms a white Butterfly whose wing is broken. The Butterfly is unconscious. The beetles carry hoes over their shoulders; some carry sickles. The Witchbeetle comes with them. All gather around. Scorpy, the Woodcutter, is collapsed on the good earth, dead drunk.

WITCHBEETLE.
> Poor wounded little butterfly.

FIELDBEETLE.
> She'll die.

WITCHBEETLE.
> There's little life left,
> but she'll be saved.

FIELDBEETLE.
> She fell from the top of an awesome cypress.
> She has a broken wing.

WITCHBEETLE.
> Poor dreaming vision,
> you know the secrets of water and flowery vales;
> how wretched to see you dying this morning,
> wept over by the sweet, prophetic nightingales.

FIELDBEETLE.

> Such pity I felt, to see her stretched out on the
> pathway.

WITCHBEETLE.

> What fortune for us, repugnant, sad-hearted,
> to caress your wings of whitest silk
> and breathe the fragrance of the gown you wear.

*Doña Beetle brings from her house some long and very
delicate leaves with which the Witchbeetle cleans the
Butterfly's wounds.*

WITCHBEETLE.

> Sweet star, fallen from a nodding cypress,
> what bitter dawn did your eyes look into as you fell?

BOYBEETLE.

> Oh, what sorrow lies deep in my soul.

SYLVIA, *to her mother, Doña Proudbeetle, who rushes in,
in a great hurry. Weeping.*

> He doesn't love me, Mother.

DOÑA PROUDBEETLE, *drily.*

> Well, what are we going to do about it?

SYLVIA.

> He loves a star now.

DOÑA PROUDBEETLE.

> Just who does he think he is,
> so painted up and ugly!

She leaves, shaking her head testily.

FIELDBEETLE.

> Look, she sighed.
> She's opening her eyes.

BUTTERFLY, *quietly, as in a dream.*

> I want to fly, I want to fly; the cord is long.

WITCHBEETLE, *to Doña Beetle.*

> Let's take her to your house.
> She's stirring from her trance.

BUTTERFLY.

> The thread stretches to the star
> where my treasure is.

My wings are made of silver.
My heart is made of gold.
The thread is dreaming
its vibrant humming sound. . . .

WITCHBEETLE.
Carry her carefully.
You might hurt her more.

The Fieldbeetles carry the Butterfly to Doña Beetle's house.

WITCHBEETLE, *to Doña Beetle.*
Give her some well-aged dew
and apply a warm poultice
of nettle paste
and lily pollen.

DOÑA BEETLE.
Will she get well, Doctoress?

WITCHBEETLE.
She'll be well soon.
In addition, I prescribe moonlight baths and naps
there in the shady nooks of the ancient wood.
Let's go in and look at her. She's beautiful!

DOÑA BEETLE.

Beautiful!

SCENE 6

THE BOYBEETLE, SCORPY THE WOODCUTTER
AND WITCHBEETLE

BOYBEETLE, *addressing his Poppy.*
Poppy, now I've seen my mysterious star.

SCORPY, *flat on his back in the meadow and as though in a chaotic limbo.*
I ate nine flies,
one lizard, one bee,
a whole beehive.

BOYBEETLE.

> My heart begins its plaint
> of a love it already feels!

WITCHBEETLE, *comes out of the little cave and goes very seriously up to the boy; then, placing a hand on his shoulder*:

> Little boy, your destiny
> hangs on the wings of this great butterfly.
> Don't look at her with hope, for then you may be
>   lost.
> Your old and ailing friend says this to you.

She makes a circle on the ground with her little stick.

> This magic circle predicts it clearly.
> If you fall in love with her, alas for you! You'll die!
> Nighttime, all of it, will crash onto your poor
>   forehead—
> the starless night in which you will be lost. . . .
> Think on this till evening.

Exits.

BOYBEETLE, *declaiming à la Don Juan.*

> What's here, inside my head?
> What skein of loves has the wind knit here for me?
> Why fades now the flower of my innocence,
> while another flower is born within my imaginings?
> Who can she be, who comes to rob me of good
>   venture
> with shaken wings, as white as ermine?
> I turn to sorrow, upon dark nighttime,
> and call my mother, as a child I called.
> O Scarlet Poppy, who o'er all the meadow gaze,
> would that I were as lovely as you.
> Comfort the sorrows of the lover, lovesick,
> weeping for the daybreak's dew.

He sits on the stone and weeps, his little head between his hands. Scorpy, the Woodcutter, gets up with difficulty and goes off, stumbling, singing in his cavernous voice.

SCORPY.

> For the little leaves of mint
> are sweet—oh my!—to pluck.
> Tatará, tatará, tatará.

The stage is full of light.

CURTAIN

ACT TWO

A garden. At the back of the stage there is a great cascade of ivy. And all the ground is to be planted with gigantic daisies. It is a real forest, but of little flowers. On Stage Left, and where it is partly lost amid the thickets, a spring's water glints. All the plants are bathed in the gentle light of deep twilight.

SCENE 1

FIRST FIELDBEETLE, SECOND FIELDBEETLE
AND SAINTBEETLE

There enter, Right, two little beetle farm women who live at the foot of some mushrooms. They are very old. One of them has the reputation, hereabouts, of being a saint.

SAINTBEETLE.

How very disgusted I am, neighbor, how disgusted. Did you see that beetle boy declaiming in the meadow?

FIRST FIELDBEETLE.

I saw him swinging himself on a spiderweb strand. He was singing sadly, sadly—dreaming, perhaps. Not a thought of earning an honest living.

SAINTBEETLE.

He's very good and very sweet. And a great poet!

FIRST FIELDBEETLE.

A loafer!
No one can earn a living on a spider strand.

SAINTBEETLE.

                                                    Neighbor,
   "Criticize thou nobody,"—so said the Great Beetle.
The other Fieldbeetle bows her antennae.
   "Consider thou thy lives as thou considerest the
       newborn grass.
   Suffer thou amongst thyselves the faults of others,
   for in My Kingdom those who sing and play are
       worthier
   than those who spend their lives at works. . . .
   For thou must be earth and thou must be water,
   petals to the rose, bark to the tree."

FIRST FIELDBEETLE.
   Of course the Great Beetle never ate, did he,
       neighbor?
Scornfully.
   Just try trying those sayings on somebody who's
       hungry.

SAINTBEETLE.
                                                      Hush!
   Hunger is a demon with antennae of fire
   whom one must exorcise by . . .

FIRST FIELDBEETLE.
                                                    Eating?

SAINTBEETLE.
                                                   Praying.

FIRST FIELDBEETLE.
   Leave me be, neighbor; you've very holy and very
       wise
   but Saint Beetle couldn't have been talking about
       this life.
   If that Boybeetle doesn't work and apply himself
   he'll starve to death—so clever and painted up.
   If I were his mother, I'd take him . . .

SAINTBEETLE.
                                                    Friend,
   his last song was of a love unattainable,

and he mentioned the wings of an injured butterfly
more worthy of the dew than a spikenard's flesh.

FIRST FIELDBEETLE.

This plague of good-for-nothings is something
   awful!

SAINTBEETLE.

Have a little pity for such a darling lover.
"Suffer upon thyselves the wounds of others,
the alien sorrows," Saint Beetle said.

FIRST FIELDBEETLE.

All that foolish mumbo jumbo is nothing to me.
And what business does he have being in love with
   a butterfly?
Doesn't he realize they can never be married?

SAINTBEETLE.

That he'll be black mire on the snow, perhaps,
that falls so white from whence we know not?

FIRST FIELDBEETLE, *forcefully.*

It falls from the lilies.

SAINTBEETLE, *severely.*

                              Don't be so sure, my friend.

FIRST FIELDBEETLE.

To put it bluntly, the Boybeetle has gone crazy!

SAINTBEETLE.

                                    He's so good.

I shall be at prayers for his rest!
His singing brings to mind my youthful love.

FIRST FIELDBEETLE, *sourly.*

Let's get on to our huts; it's late.

SAINTBEETLE, *very sadly.*

                                    Let's go.

*They both go toward the right, penetrating the ivy to
the places where their cave homes are. Night has closed
in and the first rays of the moon fall into the daisy woods.
The water of the spring trembles with a far-off tenderness.*

SCENE 2

BUTTERFLY, WITCHBEETLE, DOÑA BEETLE
AND FIELDBEETLES

The Witchbeetle and Doña Beetle, mother of the Boy-beetle, enter, Right, talking animatedly.

DOÑA BEETLE.
For our butterfly's moonbath.
this glade is very good.

WITCHBEETLE.
Her little, waxen wings
will be just as they were that lovely morning
when first she fluttered in the sunbeams.

DOÑA BEETLE.
She comes from the dawn. She's a wandering flower.
My boy said so last night.

WITCHBEETLE.
Be very careful
with your little boy, my friend.

DOÑA BEETLE.
His loving heart
sings of her at night so passionately.

WITCHBEETLE.
Then let's be on guard.

Turning to the other two and calling.

Come over here, but slowly!
Try not to let her wings scrape on the ground.
Hold her antennae—the wind is moving them,
and I'm afraid they might break off. Jump the
stream!

Coming back to Doña Beetle.

Here they are, Señora.

Enter, four Fieldbeetle women, carrying the Butterfly on their backs. To the women.

> Let her down gently, now.

To Doña Beetle.

> Did you apply the crushed fly ointment?

DOÑA BEETLE.

> Two applications.

WITCHBEETLE, *examining the butterfly*.

> She neither sees nor feels.
> Her eyes are dead, her mouth is closed.
> What realm did you come from, in your white dress?

DOÑA BEETLE, *recalling*.

> She comes from the dawn. She's a flower that flies.

WITCHBEETLE.

> You, with broken wings and wounded heart,
> retreat to those realms where love holds you still.

Addressing Doña Beetle.

> We'll leave her here, under the moon. I still hear
> the sadness of that voice within the oaken grove
> that said to me, fading off in the heart of the wind,
> "A fairy has died, the fairy of field and sea."

DOÑA BEETLE.

> Sadness or death surround my little house.
> My Boybeetle unceasingly sings of his love.

WITCHBEETLE.

> We must marry him to Sylvia right away. He needs
> to play and to forget himself.

*To one of the Fieldbeetles.**

>   Stay here in the flowers,
> Guarding over the dreams of the sleeping white
>   butterfly.
> If she sighs, hold near to her this holy branch.

DOÑA BEETLE, *back to the same theme*.

> Oh Doctoress, neighbor, my heart forewarns
> much evil.

---

* After this point these are also called Guardbeetles.—Editor.

WITCHBEETLE, *taking no notice.*
>Watch that Scorpy doesn't come.

Doña Beetle is weeping silently.

WITCHBEETLE.
>Be very patient, Señora; you're fretful.

DOÑA BEETLE, *weeping.*
>It's all, all my husband's fault.
>There's no greater misfortune than being a poet.
>I'd burn them all.

WITCHBEETLE.
>   Oblivion will burn them.

Exeunt. The stage is left deserted. The little Guardbeetle leans against the stem of a daisy and there remains motionless, except for the gentle waving of her antennae.

SCENE 3

BUTTERFLY AND GUARDBEETLES

BUTTERFLY, *beginning to awaken.*
>I'll fly along the silver thread.
>My children wait for me,
>away in the faraway fields,
>spinning at their spinning wheels.
>I am the spirit
>of silk.
>I come from a mysterious ark
>and must journey into the mist.
>Let the spider sing
>in her cave.
>Let the nightingale ponder
>my legend.
>Let the drop of rain be amazed,
>when it glides on my dead wings.
>I span away my heart on my flesh
>to pray in the darkness,

and Death gave me two white wings,
but dried up the source of my silk.
Now I understand the water's lament,
the plaint of the stars,
the plaint of the wind on the crag,
and the stinging hum
of the bee.
For I am death
and loveliness.
What the snow whispers over the fields
the hearth repeats;
the song of the smoke in the morning
is whispered by the roots beneath the ground.
But I'll fly along the silver thread.
My children are waiting for me.
Let the spider sing
in her cave;
let the nightingale ponder
my legend;
let the drop of rain be amazed,
when it glides on my dead wings.

The Butterfly slowly moves her wings.

SCENE 4

BUTTERFLY, SCORPY AND GUARDBEETLES

Scorpy's engaging pincer appears at stage right.

SCORPY.

The rich fragrance
of fresh meat
came to me.

GUARDBEETLE, *irate.*

Get away from here.

SCORPY.

Just let me look at her.

Comes nearer.

GUARDBEETLE.
> Go back to the woods, you drunk.

SCORPY.
> Wish I were.
> By now I'd have eaten
> her wings.

GUARDBEETLE.
>   Villain!
> Get out of this wood!

SCORPY, *pleadingly.*
> Just a little sample
> from where the wound is.
> Just the tip of an antenna.

GUARDBEETLE, *furiously.*
> Either you leave here right now
> or I'll call my partners
> and we'll kill you.

SCORPY, *seriously.*
>   Listen,

> if I weren't so senile
> I'd just gulp down
> your tasty skull.

Scorpy goes nearer quickly, ready to nip the Butterfly.

GUARDBEETLE, *alarmed.*
> Watch out or I'll scream. Go away!

The Butterfly moves.

> See, you're going to wake her up!

SCORPY, *jumping about and guffawing.*
> And what does the little lady,
> so tender and tempting, have to say?

GUARDBEETLE, *trying to hit Scorpy.*
> This is unbearable!

SCORPY, *very close to the Butterfly and clicking his pincers.*
> I bet you won't come near me.

GUARDBEETLE, *terrified*.

> Help! Quick, before he eats her up!

SCORPY, *backing away*.

> Shut up, you ugly bug.

GUARDBEETLE.

> Go home right now.

SCORPY, *singing cynically*.

> Back to my cave I will go.
> There I'll eat ten dead flies.

GUARDBEETLE, *outraged, pushing him*.

> Get out!

SCORPY, *teasing her*.

> Not a bad little supper!

GUARDBEETLE.

> You're stupid and evil.

SCORPY, *leaving*.

> And you're crazy and an old maid.

The Guardbeetle goes up to examine the Butterfly and then returns to her post. The brandy-roughened voice of Scorpy is heard tra-la-ing, each time farther away.

SCENE 5

FIRST FIREFLY, SECOND FIREFLY, THIRD FIREFLY
AND GUARDBEETLES

A swarm of Fireflies flicker in the grass. They slowly come nearer.

FIRST FIREFLY.

> Soon we'll be able to sip
> the dew.

THIRD FIREFLY.

> Already I've seen the lilies
> tremble in the pond.

Soon it'll fall on the grass,
clear and holy.

FIRST FIREFLY.
Will it fall from the branches
or will the cold bring it?

THIRD FIREFLY.
We shall never understand
the unknown.
My light has gone out.
I'm old and feeble.
I never saw any dew
falling from any branch.

SECOND FIREFLY.
It will spring from the earth.

THIRD FIREFLY.
A wise old man has said,
"Drink the sweet drops,
tranquil and serene,
without ever asking
from whence they come."

FIRST FIREFLY.
They make love sweet,
those drops.

THIRD FIREFLY.

We old ones

know that love
is just like the dew.
That drop you drink
is lost to the meadow
as love is lost
in the peace of forgetfulness.
Tomorrow other drops
will shine on the grass
that in a few moments
will no longer be dew.

FIRST FIREFLY.
Let's not be sad . . .

THIRD FIREFLY.

    The light I once had grew dark.

FIRST FIREFLY.

    . . . for in search of love we roam the fields.

SECOND FIREFLY.

    Soon I'll see shining
    the leaves and the earth.

FIRST FIREFLY.

    It's the fall of the dew
    that makes meadows.

*They have come very near to the Butterfly. She hears
them and murmurs as though dreaming.*

BUTTERFLY.

                                     I've heard

    how the clear drops
    spoke sweetly,
    telling the mysteries
    of boundless meadows.

THIRD FIREFLY, *brusquely turning around.*

    Drops don't talk.
    They're made to feed
    bees and glowworms.
    And they don't have souls.

BUTTERFLY.

    The grain of sand speaks,
    and the leaves of the tree.
    And all of them have
    ways of their own.
    But all their voices
    and the songs you may hear
    are strange disguises
    of a single song. A thread
    will lead me to the forests
    where Life is there to see.

THIRD FIREFLY.

    Are you by any chance a fairy?

BUTTERFLY.

> I don't know what I've been.
> I shed my heart
> and my soul little by little
> and now my poor body
> is dead and empty.

FIRST FIREFLY.

> Well, then, enjoy love,
> for the morning is coming.
> Drink, in all joy,
> the drops of the dew.

BUTTERFLY.

> I don't know what love is,
> nor shall I ever know.

FIRST FIREFLY.

> Love is the kiss
> in the quiet nest
> while the leaves are trembling,
> mirrored in the water.

BUTTERFLY.

> My wings are broken
> and my body is cold.

FIRST FIREFLY.

> But you can still kiss
> and move your antennae.

BUTTERFLY.

> Oh, but I have no mouth!

FIRST FIREFLY.

> Your frock is lovely.

BUTTERFLY.

> What are you—stars?

FIRST FIREFLY.

> We seek a lover,
> and drunk with love
> we travel the roads.

BUTTERFLY.

> I don't know what love is.
> Why do you disturb my sleep?

THIRD FIREFLY.

> We'll leave you in peace.
> Be very happy!

BUTTERFLY.

>   The thread
> of silver leads to meadows
> where Life is to be seen.

The Fireflies leave, commenting as they retire.

FIRST FIREFLY.

> Could she be a fairy?

SECOND FIREFLY.

>   Her body
> is completely asleep.

FIRST FIREFLY.

> It frightens me to look at her,
> so white, so all alone.

THIRD FIREFLY.

> She's a butterfly,
> half-dead with cold.

SECOND FIREFLY.

> What a great mystery;
> let's go back to our field.

THIRD FIREFLY.

> And let our burning bodies
> call to love.
> Ah, to entwine one's self
> with a strong lover.

FIRST FIREFLY, *intrigued.*

> Why did she say
> that dewdrops talk?

The Fireflies are gradually lost.

SCENE 6

BUTTERFLY, THE BOYBEETLE, GUARDBEETLES,
AND WITCHBEETLE

*The other little Fieldbeetle woman walks back and forth
across the stage. The Boybeetle appears, most charmingly
painted yellow. He wears a tormented look.*

BOYBEETLE, *declamatorily*.
> The foliage and the flowers
> were fading.
> About me I held the stillness
> of the morn.

FIELDBEETLE, *irritatedly*.
> (Now here we have it,
> just what we needed.)
> He's daubed himself with lily pollen
> so she'll love him.

BOYBEETLE.
> 'Twas the joyous time of my tranquil verse.
> But to my threshhold a fairy
> has come, clad in transparent snow
> to steal my soul away.
> What, in these meadows, shall I do without love,
>   without kisses?
> Shall I fling myself to the waves?
> But I ponder the world of my mother's dreams,
> a world of bliss beyond these boughs,
> full of nightingales, full of boundless meadows,
> the world of dew,
> where love is unceasing.
> But what if Saint Beetle does not exist? To what
>   end
> my fatal bitterness? Above these boughs,
> doesn't Someone watch over us, who can make us
> superior to all creation?

FIELDBEETLE.

> Too bad.
> Definitely, completely crazy.

SCENE 7

BUTTERFLY, THE BOYBEETLE, GUARDBEETLES
AND WITCHBEETLE

BOYBEETLE, *going up close to the Butterfly.*

> The chaste queen of this meadow sleeps?
> She whom the dew bedecks?
> She who knows the secret of the leaves
> and the song of the waters?

The Butterfly does not answer, but starts to dance.

> You do not answer me. Perhaps you did not hear
> my impassioned voice?

The Butterfly moves as if trying to fly.

> Do you want to fly? There's much darkness above,
> and you have a broken wing.
> I'll heal your wounds with kisses
> if you'll marry me.
> And a great, great nightingale who is my friend
> will take us flying in the dawn.
> Don't keep on trying to fly. It's nighttime. See
> how dark it is among the branches.
> Darkness is the weight that makes us sleep.
> It's very subtle and overwhelming.

The Butterfly falls to the ground.

> Without you my heart is withering.

The Boybeetle goes to her.

> Pay heed to my words.
> Don't think of flying toward the mountains,
> but stay here in my house.

I'll catch for your delight
a good cricket
who will lull you to sleep at night
and at daybreak
I'll bring you pebbles from the pond,

The Guardbeetle goes between the stems of the daisies
in order to hear better.

little dwarf ants,
and you'll drink the dewdrops
from my burning lips.
What have I seen in your antennae,
Butterfly? Fairies' mirror,
you're like a flower from another world,
or like water's foam.

The Boybeetle is clasping the Butterfly. She surrenders
herself to him unknowingly.

Your body is cold. Come with me,
for my den is warm
and from it you'll see the green meadow
stretch into the distance.

The Butterfly withdraws suddenly and dances.

Have you no heart? Has not the fire
of my words set you aflame?
Then whom shall I tell my sorrows to?
Oh, enchanted poppy!
Mother of the dew on my meadow.
Why, if water may have
cool shadow in summer, if the dark
of night is lightened
by the endless winking of the stars,
cannot my soul have love?
Who gave me these eyes I hate?
And these hands that try
to clutch a love I cannot understand
and that will end with my life?
Who has lost me among shadows?
Who bids me suffer because I have no wings?

GUARDBEETLE.
>   Oh, why do you shout so, Boybeetle?
>   He's gone mad!

WITCHBEETLE.
>   What's happened?

(*Manuscript ends here.*)

MUSIC FOR THE SONGS

The following music for songs in the plays in this volume is that of their original productions, as far as actors who took part in the plays and others close to Federico García Lorca have been able to reconstruct it. Some of this music he composed himself; some he wrote down from folk airs that had not been, we believe, previously collected. It should be remembered that García Lorca was trained in music from childhood. His close friendship with the older Manuel de Falla was cemented by their common enthusiasm for Spain's sophisticated as well as primitive musical heritage.

Certain of the music for these plays first appeared in print in *Federico García Lorca (1899–1936)*, New York, Hispanic Institute of the United States, 1941, a volume long out-of-print. This music has been reproduced without change in the successive editions of *Obras Completas* of Federico García Lorca, published by Aguilar, Madrid. In 1961 Union Musical Espanola of Madrid (Carrera de San Jeronimo 26 y Adrenal 18, but represented in the United States by Associated Music Publishers, 1 West 47th Street, New York 17), published *Canciones de Teatro de García Lorca* by Gustavo Pittaluga, a friend of the playwright and a composer of note. It includes many more of these songs, scored for the piano or guitar by Pittaluga and will be very helpful to producers and students.

However, the music given here, which includes three songs not previously published, was written down in New York with the help particularly of Francisco García Lorca, Laura García Lorca de los Rios, Gustavo Duran and Wolfgang Sauerlander, to whom the publishers are deeply grateful.

For the final version of the translations of the poems, which had to be reworked so that they could fit the music, the publishers take full responsibility.

The music for *Doña Rosita, The Spinster* was not especially written for the play and is set to tunes easily available. The music for *The Butterfly's Evil Spell* has not survived, but if it can ever be reconstructed, we will publish it in successive editions to this book.

R.M.M.

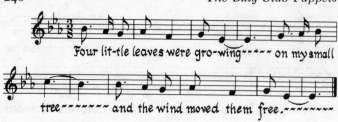

Four lit~tle leaves were gro~wing~~~~~ on my small

tree~~~~~~~ and the wind moved them free.~~~~~~~

Andante

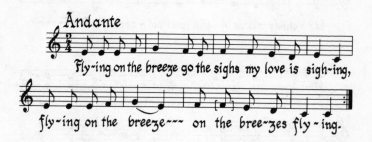

Fly~ing on the breeze go the sighs my love is sigh~ing,

fly~ing on the breeze~~~ on the bree~zes fly~ing.

Allegretto

Oh this vi~to, vi~to thrills me~~~~ and I'll
       vi~to, vi~to, vi~to~~~~ with this

dance it till it kills me~~~ with this
vi~to that I   hum you;~~~Eve~ry

hour, oh~~~~~~~~my dar~ling~~~~ I go
mo~ment~~~deep de~sire~~~~~~~~ sets me

far~ther, far~ther from you;~~~~for each
more and more on   fire.~~~~~~~~~~~~~~~

The speck-le-dy bird was a ~ sit ~ ting, sit ~ ting on the green lem~on tree.~~~~ With her beak and her tail she

stirred the leaves and blos~soms so an~xi~ous~ly. When?

Oh,~~~~~ when my love shall I see?~~~~~~~

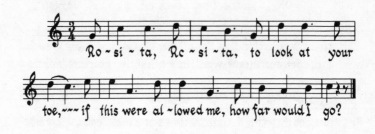

Ro ~ si ~ ta, Ro ~ si ~ ta, to look at your

toe,~~~ if this were al~lowed me, how far would I go?

U ~ ri me ~ men ~ to. A man is dead.~~~

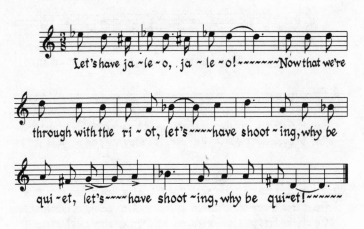

Let's have ja~le~o, ja~le~o! ~~~~~~~Now that we're

through with the ri~ot, let's~~~~have shoot~ing, why be

qui~et, let's~~~~have shoot~ing, why be qui~et!~~~~~~

If your mo~~ther~~wants a king,~~~~~~In the
Di~a~monds, Clubs and Hearts,~~~~King of

deck~~~~~~~~~~~there's a store.~~~~~~King of
Spades~~~~~~~~~~that makes four!~~~~~

Polka

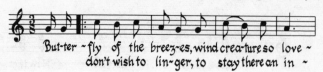

But~ter ~fly of the breez~es, wind crea~ture so love ~
don't wish to lin~ger, to stay there an in ~

ly; but~ter~fly of the breez~es, wind crea~ture so love ~ly; but~ter~
stant. But you don't wish to lin~ger, to stay there an in~stant. But~ter

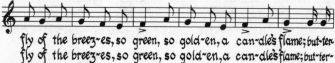

fly of the breez~es, so green, so gold~en, a can~dle's flame; but~ter
fly of the breez~es, so green, so gold~en, a can~dle's flame; but~ter~

fly of the breez~es, I beg you stay there, stay there, stay there! But you
fly of the breez~es, I beg you stay there, stay there, stay

there! I beg you, stay there! But~ter~fly, oh, please, are you there?

Allegretto e ben marcato

Mis~tress Cob~bler, Mis~tress Cob~bler, since her
Turned her house in~to a tav~ern where the

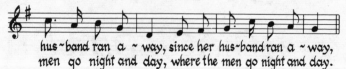

hus~band ran a ~ way, since her hus~band ran a ~way,
men go night and day, where the men go night and day.

Note: Gustavo Pittaluga gives a comical trumpet flourish which could be
used here, although it is not believed to be related to the original one.
Almost any trumpet flourish, slightly off key and comical, lasting 15 to 20
seconds, would do.   —Editor

Ah, love, ah love. Tight in my warm thighs im-pri-soned,
Ah, love, ah love. Morn-ing cock, the night is go-ing!

there swims like a fish, the sun.~~~~~~~~~~~~~~~~~
Please don't let it van-ish, no! ~~~~~~~~~~~~~~~~~

Tight~~~in my thighs im-pris-oned~~~there swims like a fish the

sun. Oh, love, oh, love. Oh, love, oh love, oh love. Oh, love~~~~

warm wa-ter in the ru-shes.~~~ Morn-ing cock, the night is

go-ing! Love, oh love, oh, love. Don't let it van-ish, no!

Note: In an interview Federico García Lorca gave in 1933 he said:
"The work [*Don Perlimplín*] is embedded in music like a chamber opera.
All the short intermissions are tied together by sonatas of Scarlatti, and
the dialogue is constantly emphasized by chords and musical background."

Gustavo Pittaluga provides a sonata for the prologue in the manner of
Scarlatti. It is believed that in the first performances an actual Scarlatti
sonata was used.

—Editor

U - pon the banks of the ri~ver~~~~~~~~ the

pas~sing night paused to bathe,~~~ the pas~sing night

paused to   bathe.~~~~~ And on the breasts of Be~

li~sa~~~~~~~~ the flowers lan~guish of their love~~

the flowers lan~guish of their love.~~~~~~~~~~

New Directions Paperbooks

Henry Miller,
  Remember to Remember. NDP111.
  The Smile at the Foot of the Ladder.
    NDP176.
  The Time of the Assassins. NDP115.
  The Wisdom of the Heart. NDP94.
Yukio Mishima, *Death in Midsummer.*
  NDP215.
Eugenio Montale, *Selected Poems.*† NDP193.
Vladimir Nabokov, *Nikolai Gogol.* NDP78.
New Directions 17. (Anthology) NDP103.
New Directions 18. (Anthology) NDP163.
New Directions 19. (Anthology) NDP214.
Charles Olson, *Selected Writings.* NDP231.
George Oppen,
  The Materials. (SFR) NDP122.
  This In Which. (SFR) NDP201.
Wilfred Owen, *Collected Poems.* NDP210.
Boris Pasternak, *Safe Conduct.* NDP77.
Kenneth Patchen, *Because It Is.* NDP83.
  Doubleheader. NDP211.
  Hallelujah Anyway. NDP219.
  The Journal of Albion Moonlight. NDP99.
  Memoirs of a Shy Pornographer. NDP205.
  Selected Poems. NDP160.
Plays for a New Theater. (Anthology)
  NDP216.
Ezra Pound, *ABC of Reading.* NDP89.
  Classic Noh Theatre of Japan. NDP79.
  The Confucian Odes. NDP81.
  Confucius to Cummings. (Anthology)
    NDP126.
  Love Poems of Ancient Egypt. Gift Edition.
    NDP178.
  Selected Poems. NDP66.
  Translations.† (Enlarged Edition) NDP145.
Philip Rahv, *Image and Idea.* NDP67.
Herbert Read, *The Green Child.* NDP208.
Jesse Reichek, *Etcetera.* NDP196.
Kenneth Rexroth, *Assays.* NDP113.
  Bird in the Bush. NDP80.
  The Homestead Called Damascus. WPS3.
  Natural Numbers. (Selected Poems)
    NDP141.
  100 Poems from the Chinese. NDP192.
  100 Poems from the Japanese.† NDP147.
Charles Reznikoff,
  By the Waters of Manhattan. (SFR)
    NDP121.

Charles Reznikoff,
  Testimony: The United States 1885–1890.
    (SFR) NDP200.
Arthur Rimbaud, *Illuminations.*† NDP56.
  Season in Hell & Drunken Boat.† NDP97.
San Francisco Review Annual No. 1.
  (SFR) NDP138.
Jean-Paul Sartre, *Baudelaire.* NDP233.
  Nausea. NDP82.
Stevie Smith, *Selected Poems.* NDP159.
Stendhal, *Lucien Leuwen.*
  Book I: *The Green Huntsman.* NDP107.
  Book II: *The Telegraph.* NDP108.
Jules Supervielle, *Selected Writings.*† NDP209.
Dylan Thomas, *Adventures in the Skin Trade.*
  NDP183.
  A Child's Christmas in Wales. Gift Edition.
    NDP181.
  Portrait of the Artist as a Young Dog.
    NDP51.
  Quite Early One Morning. NDP90.
  Under Milk Wood. NDP73.
Norman Thomas, *Ask at the Unicorn.*
  NDP129.
Lionel Trilling, *E. M. Forster.* NDP189.
Paul Valéry, *Selected Writings.*† NDP184.
Vernon Watkins, *Selected Poems.* NDP221.
Nathanael West, *Miss Lonelyhearts &*
  Day of the Locust. NDP125.
George F. Whicher, tr.,
  The Goliard Poets.† NDP206.
Tennessee Williams,
  The Glass Menagerie. NDP218.
  Hard Candy. NDP225.
  In the Winter of Cities. NDP154.
  27 Wagons Full of Cotton. NDP217.
William Carlos Williams,
  The Autobiography. NDP223.
  The Farmers' Daughters. NDP106.
  In the American Grain. NDP53.
  Many Loves. NDP191.
  Paterson. Complete. NDP152.
  Pictures from Brueghel. NDP118.
  Selected Poems. NDP131.
  White Mule. NDP226.
Curtis Zahn,
  American Contemporary. (SFR) NDP139.

(SFR) A New Directions / San Francisco Review Book.   † Bilingual.

**Complete descriptive catalog available free on request from
New Directions, 333 Sixth Avenue, New York 10014.**